THE PENNINE CYCLEW

NORTHERN SECTION
KENDAL TO BERWICK UPON TWEED

TED LIDDLE

DALESMAN

Dalesman Publishing Company Ltd

Stable Courtyard, Broughton Hall,
Skipton, North Yorkshire BD23 3AZ
www.dalesman.co.uk

First published 2003

Maps: Jeremy Ashcroft

A British Library Cataloguing in Publication record
is available for this book

ISBN 1 85568 206-0

Printed in China by Midas Printing International Limited

FOREWORD BY JOHN GRIMSHAW DIRECTOR & CHIEF ENGINEER, SUSTRANS

With this book in your hand you have a sure guide to some of the most glorious cycling in the country. You can forget the frustrations of battling with traffic in congested towns, of devising shortcuts to avoid the worst of the conflict, of being surrounded by hard surfaces and constant noise – and exchange it all for space, clean air, distant views, the sound of some remote bird and the challenge of the hills.

This is the place to recharge your batteries, to be confirmed in the wonderful splendour of cycling in its light touch over the ground, and to go home refreshed to cycle more for everyday journeys. It is our ambition in Sustrans to bring about a real increase in cycling as the one truly sustainable form of transport suitable for many types of trip.

The whole Pennine Cycleway is the result of a most productive partnership of local authorities who manage the route, funding bodies including the Countryside Agency, supportive landowners and committed local cyclists, all of whom we thank for their key contributions.

Ted Liddle has done a magnificent job in making this National Cycle Network Route 68 accessible to all, and we salute his dedication and knowledge, and hope that as you end your ride you will appreciate that you have been in the hands of a genuine routemaster. Do not stop now, but continue and follow the spectacular southern section from Derby to Kendal!

JOHN GRIMSHAW, April 2003

PHOTOGRAPHIC ACKNOWLEDGEMENTS

Val Corbett   (pages 36, 48 and 51)
John Grimshaw   (pages 5 and 72)
David Tarn   (pages 58 and 92)
All other photographs by Ted Liddle

Front cover   The Cheviots, Upper Coquetdale by Alan Wilson
Back cover   *Clockwise from left*:
                   Looking towards the North Pennines, Ted Liddle
                   The Eden Valley, Val Corbett
                   Rutter Force, Ted Liddle
                   Berwick upon Tweed, David Tarn

PREFACE BY TED LIDDLE

There are now three Pennine 'ways' which follow the backbone of England from the Peak District up to the Scottish Borders.

The original **Pennine Way** is the long distance *walking* route originated by Tom Stephenson, popularised in the books of Alfred Wainwright and now almost a national institution. A National Trail designed for walkers, it uses various categories of rights of way. After an initial period of excessive wear and tear, it is now being maintained and appropriately managed for the nation's continued use and enjoyment.

The Pennine Bridleway is a long distance *equestrian* route beginning at Middleton Top in Derbyshire and finishing at Byrness, a small village in Northumberland on the English side of the Scottish border. This too is a National Trail. The southern half ends at the Fat Lamb Inn near Kirkby Stephen in Cumbria. The northern extension received approval from the Secretary of State in 2002 and the implementation process will follow in due course. Cyclists and walkers will be able to use this route as of legal right though, as it is designed for horseriders, it will not always be ideal for cyclists.

The author en route to Bellingham

The Pennine Cycleway is a long distance cycle route created principally for *cyclists*. It more or less follows the same alignment as the Pennine Bridleway but uses existing quiet minor roads, country lanes and, only where necessary, a variety of suitable off-road tracks. It is part of the 10,000 mile National Cycle Network, shown on maps as NCN Route 68, and passes through high quality, attractive and varied scenery including the Peak, Yorkshire Dales and Northumberland National Parks, the North Pennines Area of Outstanding Natural Beauty and Kielder Forest. The southern section of the Pennine Cycleway begins in Derbyshire and meets the northern section in the Lune Gorge with a link route to/from Kendal for ease of arrival and/or onward transport. The northern section of the Pennine Cycleway ends at Berwick upon Tweed. The route north of Appleby was opened in July 2002.

This is the definitive guidebook for the Pennine Cycleway (North) written by its original route surveyor working as part of the Sustrans team which developed the whole length of the Pennine Cycleway. But it is more than a guidebook; it is a detailed compilation of route and area knowledge that reflects and embodies the author's love and knowledge of the countryside through which the route passes. It has been written with the great affection a father has for his young offspring so read on and discover this superb route for yourself.

TED LIDDLE, April 2003

CONTENTS

KEY: Text

R: right

L: left

TR: turn right

TL: turn left

SA: straight ahead

X-rds: crossroads

T-j: T junction

(L) (R): on your left/right

PH: pub

LC: level crossing

DRT: disused railway track

DAP: dismount and push!

PCW: Pennine Cycleway

NCN: National Cycle Network

CRs: cycle routes

CCW Cumbria Cycleway

KEY: Maps

———	Main road route
··········	Route option
———	Off road route
———	Other cycle routes
··············	Take care for section of road
▶	Recommended direction of travel
>	Steep hill (points downhill)
▷	Junction. Take care
☕	Pub/Cafe
🛏	Accommodation
▲	Hostel
S	Shop
🚲	Cycle shop
i	Information
T	Telephone
🚻	Toilets

INTRODUCTION

OVERALL ROUTE SUMMARY

The Pennine Cycleway (North) is best started from Kendal which can be easily reached by mainline railway and/or motorway. Quiet country roads then lead through beautiful scenery towards Kirkby Stephen and the eastern reaches of the Eden Valley. The heather-clad North Pennines are then crossed using part of the established C2C Cycle Route before reaching the little-known Upper South Tyne Valley linking Alston with Haltwhistle – just two of several interesting, if not unique, en route 'market towns'.

The central section is highly scenic with strong historical connections. Between the Tyne Valley and Redesdale, the PCW climbs past numerous Roman settlements to give impressive views of Hadrian's Wall, Kielder Forest and vast expanses of Northumberland's unspoilt landscape. This is a challenging and varied section of route characterised by solitude and beautiful scenery.

The most northern section of the route passes through the amazingly peaceful Cheviot Hills where there are two options – either to the north, with sections of off-road route, or to the south which is all on tarmac and almost as scenic. The PCW then skirts the eastern flanks of the Cheviots to Wooler, again with some off-road options, after which the hills are left behind before briefly entering Scotland. This is the Tweed Valley and the route now shares NCN Route 1 for the very pleasant entry into Berwick upon Tweed, with its mainline railway and A1 trunk road, where the route ends.

The PCW can be cycled in either direction but it is probably best done south to north to take advantage of the prevailing south-westerly wind and to enjoy the increasingly remote 'feel' which the northbound journey invokes. The PCW will undoubtedly become different things to different people but to most it will be a challenge, an adventure, an achievement and a remarkable memory. Though not of Patagonian proportions, this is precisely why the Pennine Cycleway may well raise the profile of cycle touring in the same way that the Pennine Way did for walking.

ON-ROAD AND OFF-ROAD OPTIONS

The route is mainly on-road but the further north you go the more off-road options appear. The reason the route is braided is to satisfy those cyclists who prefer to do their cycling as much as possible on tarmac whilst meeting the needs of those whose preference is to cycle off-road whenever possible. There is some signing to make this obvious but unfortunately this is not always the case so combining judicious map-reading with planning ahead is the key. The criteria for choosing which sections are to be included as a braid are somewhat flexible but, in all cases, the off-road sections are legal, viable, cyclable and highly enjoyable. This should mean that, with or without luggage, daily progress is not impeded by technical difficulties.

MAPS

The sketch maps in this guidebook show the main route plus various options. For the off-road sections it is strongly recommended that you use these maps in conjunction with relevant OS maps. It could take as many as 9 Landranger maps to cover the entire route between Kendal and Berwick upon Tweed if the Carlisle feeder is included, i.e. numbers 97, 91, 90, 86, 85, 87, 80, 81 and 75. As each OS map is updated, the NCN and the PCW will be shown but this will take a number of years. In this guidebook, the on-road route is marked in red whilst the off-road sections are highlighted in green. Blue is used to denote other designated cycle routes. At the time of writing, Sustrans have produced a panelled map for the all-tarmac route as signed between Appleby and Berwick and a further map which includes Kendal to Appleby. Maps are planned to follow for the southern route sections. A compass is essential on the off-road route between the A68 and Chew Green via the open fells as described in Stage 4B.

SIGNAGE

At the time of going to press, the PCW was not yet signed between Kendal and Appleby, which is why the travel directions are more detailed for this section. North of Appleby, there is a level of en route signage as deemed appropriate by both relevant Highway departments who, it has to be said, are not always best experienced at seeing the world through the eyes of a travelling cyclist. The signs in Cumbria show the letters PCW and route number 68 whilst in Northumberland only route number 68 is displayed. In mid-Northumberland north of Alwinton, there are a couple of signed route variations but there is no information as to which is the main route, which is the variant and why. Intersection with and sharing other cycle routes happens on several occasions but more often than not the signing as it currently exists leaves the touring cyclist with an unnecessary amount of detective work. These problems should be rectified in due course but are worth mentioning in case progress is slow.

USING THIS GUIDEBOOK

This guidebook is full of interesting and useful information about the PCW (North) over and above travel directions. It has been written on the assumption that most people will use it to cycle the route from Kendal to Berwick upon Tweed (south to north) in either one continuous journey or perhaps over two, or even three, short breaks. The other option is to use the PCW route alignment to create a number of day rides utilising public transport or self-made loops. It is now generally accepted that 'a route is not a product' and, in order to enjoy the experience of cycling the PCW with an acceptable degree of anticipated fulfilment and pleasure, there needs to be a support system of cycle-friendly services. New routes do not have a full range of relevant services in place when they are created; these evolve in response to the demand stimulated by increased route usage. This is why route planning in advance is so important.

TEXT

All relevant route information is presented in a relaxed and informal style with the assumption that the guide will be usefully read at the planning stage, prior to departure, en route as and when required, and post-route to rekindle fond memories! Travel directions take priority but 'points of interest' are included in italics at the appropriate locations. Additional 'local interest' information has been slotted in where space permits as well as a 'tip of the day'. These are worth noting as several of the tips will almost certainly prove very useful during the journey! Guideline distances between identified locations are bracketed in the text.

THE PLANNING PROCESS: 'Discover, decide, book and go'

In order to make sure you take advantage of the full PCW (North) 'experience' you must 'discover, decide, book and go'. This guidebook is designed to make that process as simple as possible. Obviously you have already 'discovered' the existence of the PCW because you are reading this book but its prime purpose is to help you 'discover' the relevant information you need to 'decide' how you will cycle the route and how this can be best achieved. Booking the required services before you 'go' is not an essential prerequisite but an option most people choose in order to remove all avoidable uncertainties. As cycle accreditation (a cycle-friendly quality assurance scheme for en route service providers) becomes the accepted norm, advance bookings can be made with the confidence that, in terms of support-services, expectations will be met.

RESEARCHING ROUTE INFORMATION

Apart from this guidebook, the main sources for route information are the Sustrans map/guide – mail order 0845 113 0065, www.nationalcyclenetwork.org.uk and a new website www.penninecycleway.info which is under development. The information it contains will grow along with the route's popularity which in turn will generate new services and features on the site. Principal information sources and contact details are included in the appropriate sections of this guide.

Approaching Tarn Moor, east of Orton

PLANNING

DOING THE ROUTE: The decision process

Once you have decided to cycle the route, the next stage is a simple but essential one in which you will need to make a series of informed decisions. Ask yourself *when* you want to tackle the route, with *whom*, in *which* direction and on *what* cycle? You will also need to assess your fitness level, *how* you are to get to the start of the route and back home once you've finished, your daily distance – whether this will be on-road or off-road – your key 'staging posts' and type of accommodation required including availability and price and whether this will be pre-booked or 'take a chance'. Also, will you carry luggage or arrange its delivery, be independent or book with a specialist company, include on or off-route visits or just do the route? You will also need to check out the location of en route support services, research route information and so on.

PREPARATION

If you are not a frequent cyclist but intend to do the PCW as a special event then it is important that you cycle regularly leading up to departure. Apart from being good for your health and the environment, cycling on a regular basis provides the basis on which

to build stamina and cycle-awareness. Gradually increase the mileage over two to three months making sure you include hills as your fitness level improves. Perfect the art of pedalling and changing gear smoothly so that your personal cadence becomes natural and automatic. (Cadence is maximum forward momentum produced from optimum pedal revolutions using minimum amount of energy which results in minimal wastage of effort.) You will know when you have got it right because cycling will be easier, your progress much smoother and you will feel less tired. Additionally, you will be able to change the chain across both the front and rear cogs fluently and effortlessly *using both gear levers simultaneously*. And of course, as you become fitter, you will have to dismount and push less frequently (everyone does so at some juncture!) AND you will recover faster after hilly sections. Remember, if you learn to cycle up most hills then you will find you CAN cycle up most hills!

There is no substitute for going cycling to become cycle fit and this is the best method of avoiding 'numb bum' syndrome. This is no joke and at its worst can totally ruin the whole trip for you and your companions. Getting your 'derriere' cycle-fit is as important as getting your legs and lungs fit. Ignore this advice and you will soon become a cycling dinosaur (a megasaurars)!

TRAVEL TO/FROM THE ROUTE

The train Cycling is probably the most environmentally-friendly method of transport known to mankind and it is well worth considering making the *whole* experience of cycling the PCW as pollution-free as possible. With the necessary amount of pre-planning and advance booking, it is not difficult to travel to and from the route by means of public transport thereby reducing rural congestion and the impact of what cycling the PCW is an escape from – the motor car Although Kendal has its own station on the Windermere line, Oxenholme – The Lake District – on the outskirts of the town – is the station to use as it lies on the main West Coast line. Berwick is on the East Coast mainline. Advance booking is essential if you are to travel on the train with your cycle and doing so well in advance will obtain the best value price. Ask for details on 08457 48 49 50 or book online at www.thetrainline.com

Private vehicles For those to whom car travel is genuinely unavoidable, Kendal does not yet offer supervised car parking but this will inevitably become available when demand reaches a critical point. The M6 is the obvious travel corridor reducing car pressure on minor roads. Another option is to consider hiring a minibus with its own cycle trailer for groups of cyclists.

Support vehicles Larger groups and charity events regrettably all too often use support vehicles on long-distance cycle routes, but are they really appropriate? Surely total self-sufficiency without the need for such vehicles adds an extra layer of satisfaction to the adventure. In terms of the environment and the quality of the experience, cycling without reliance on vehicles makes complete sense and cycling without the encumbrance from such vehicles is every cyclist's right. For those groups who have convinced themselves that the use of a support vehicle is absolutely essential, the following code has been devised:

1 Ask yourself if the use of a support vehicle is really necessary
2 If so deemed and you have identified the unquestionable benefits and the beneficiaries, balance these perceived advantages against the costs to the environment, the route experience for the party, other cyclists and local people
3 Avoid driving the support vehicle ON the route unless in an emergency as this spoils the route experience for everyone else and disturbs and upsets local residents
4 Meet up with cyclists being 'supported' on a minimal/essential basis only
5 Drive to these minimal/essential meeting points using main roads and not habitually *along* the cycle route – do not 'shadow' the cycling party
6 Keep in audio contact by mobile phone rather than with the

support vehicle itself if regular contact is thought to be so important
7 Park in totally safe locations at all times not ON or blocking the route and remove ALL litter including fruit skins which take many months to biodegrade
8 In any event, encourage the party to purchase food and supplies from local shops on or close to route sources – importing such items from distant supermarkets contributes nothing to the local economy and only justifies the use of a support vehicle
9 If the vehicle is to be used only for luggage transfer then look at the alternatives; use panniers or a saddle bag, arrange with en route accommodations to transfer your luggage for you, take less gear and choose with care the gear you do take
10 Remember, this may be *your* only visit but that is also true of cyclists who wish to cycle unconstrained by vehicles. Your support vehicle may be unique to your trip but almost certainly it won't be a unique experience for en route local residents.

DAILY MILEAGE

This guide splits the PCW into six chapters which describe five route sections linking small market towns along its length. Stages 4A and 4B cover the same route section but describe two different options. The route can be done in five days following this framework and using the market towns as accommodation bases. However, some will find the daily 'chapter' distances too great and others too short – the choice is yours.

The **distances** cycled each day are largely determined by the nature of the terrain – which is often wild and remote – and services available. There are, however, numerous hamlets and off-route villages along the way that offer accommodation which could allow you to reduce or increase your daily distances. This will obviously require you to do some extra homework beforehand.

The **terrain** over which the route passes varies enormously and, of course, what goes up invariably comes down. The North Pennines, Hadrian's Wall Country, the Northumberland National Park and the Cheviots all have one thing in common – hills. It is the hills which make the PCW so distinctive, but there is plenty of easy-going terrain between and even through the hilly sections, such is the route's design.

By and large, daily cycle **time** equates to daily cycling distance but there are means by which this can be influenced for better or worse. Some obvious factors have already been covered but cycle choice and condition, terrain, weather, fitness, diet, water intake, clothing, companions, determination and speed are all relevant factors.

Perhaps the importance of **'rhythm and flow'** is the one factor which people fail to fully recognise because it is one of those things which is only obvious once it has been pointed out. *'Rhythm and flow' can be described as rate of progress in relation to the number of stops and starts during the available cycling time or journey.* The ability to maintain 'rhythm and flow' whilst cycling has a direct bearing on 'available' time, opportunity, energy and propensity for enjoyment and, ultimately, personal satisfaction without which good memories are rarely associated. Stops are important and there are many reasons why they have to be made. Too many, however, lengthen the journey by increasing the time taken; they inhibit good progress, prevent assimilating a good breathing rhythm and they frustrate – especially those stops which are unnecessary and avoidable.

The **weather** is the one variable which cannot be controlled. Temperature affected by sun, rain, or both, is always relevant but wind speed and direction are probably the two most important meteorological factors. South-west is the prevailing wind direction which is why this guide is written from Kendal to Berwick upon Tweed. Not only does this direction increase the likelihood of a tailwind but it means the sun is always at your back. Too much sun is energy sapping, causes sunburn and dramatically increases inevitable dehydration. Not enough sun tends to have a negative effect on most people but some more than others. So plan ahead to take account of all variations.

Rain is always an outside risk – literally! Accept its likelihood and prepare accordingly by adopting the right frame of mind and carrying the right clothing (see later section). The combination of a headwind and rain is the worst to overcome as this invariably provides a strong test of character, machine, gear and clothing. Wind and rain nearly always knock best-laid plans and your level of enjoyment for six; the combination will reveal any areas where your preparation is weak and your choices ill-considered. Fortunately, on most occasions, this rarely proves more than inconvenient although watching the forecast is never a waste of time. There is just no substitute for experience which is the reservoir from which all these recommendations are drawn.

EN ROUTE SERVICE PROVIDERS

There are seven types of en route service provider of which you should be aware to make your cycle tour complete. The two main ones are 'loos and brews – teas and pees' but the complete set comprises: serviced and unserviced accommodation, refreshments, visitor attractions, relevant shops, art and craft places (often with tearooms), transport and, lastly, general needs – Tourist Information Centres (TICs), public toilets, telephones, cashpoints and info about

emergency assistance for you or your bike. The quality of your journey is dependent on how easy it is to access each one of these service providers as and when you wish to do so. You may not need to access all of them but almost certainly you will be using most of them at some point. You will know when the PCW has become truly cycle-friendly when all seven categories are switched on and tuned in to your presence and each and every one of them is easy to find and set up to serve cyclists. Homework done in advance will greatly assist your awareness of visitor attractions and sites worth seeing.

ACCOMMODATION

This guide uses existing small market towns as stopover points but the countryside in between also offers a range of accommodation. This includes hotels, guest houses, B&Bs, bunkbarns, camping barns and campsites. To find these places you must either visit www. penninecycleway.info or send for the local holiday accommodation guides.

Other long-distance CRs suggest that the full range of above accommodation types are used by touring cyclists. It seems that most people on a cycle touring holiday prefer to stay in Bed & Breakfast accommodation and there is evidence to suggest that multi-night return visits for a further centre-based cycling holiday are not unusual. Cycle Accreditation is gradually arriving which means the standard of services offered to touring cyclists is appropriate and the understanding of what the term 'cycle-friendly' means is universally practised. New CRs take a little time to become really cycle-friendly and this process is quickened by volume of demand.

You can book before you go or as you go. The former saves time, trouble and anxiety but commits to given distances. The latter suits the free spirit but can cause avoidable stress, particularly during high season periods. An additional 'paid for' service is luggage transfer by advance arrangement with your accommodation providers. Whilst this is a good idea, it is not yet an established practice. Asking for this service will speed up its availability.

Several cycle tour operators will take care of the whole process for you including cycle hire, accommodation, luggage transfer and insurance. Just luggage transfer is an option offered by some. The Package Holiday approach is very sociable as you meet up with like-minded people all sharing the same journey which is an attractive idea to some. This option also takes away the need to advance plan your cycle tour in great detail which again appeals to some but not others.

CHILDREN

Because of the hills and the remote countryside through which the route passes, the PCW is a challenge route and unsuitable for small children. Some older fitter children will manage, given encouragement, reasonable weather, acceptable daily distances and no luggage to carry. The ability and determination to cycle sensible daily distances for a number of consecutive days are the main prerequisites but also taking account of all the factors outlined in this section.

EQUIPMENT

YOUR CYCLE

Your cycle needs to be the right size for you, well maintained and in good condition. It should be serviced a couple of weeks before the ride to allow time for minor adjustments and so that new parts can be 'run in' before departure. Pay particular attention to new cables which will stretch after a few days and invariably need adjusting. Booking a pre-route service immediately prior to the ride without a decent test ride is rarely a good idea.

It is not too difficult to avoid discomfort and/or pain which results from doing a cycle ride which is longer and more arduous than you are used to. This involves putting in the miles over a period of time beforehand and, most importantly, making sure your cycle is set up for your height, weight and build. If this is not addressed then you will suffer needlessly regardless of your personal fitness. Make friends with your local cycle dealer and ask his/her advice about frame size, handlebar height and design including grips and bar ends, length of handlebar extension, saddle design, angle, position and height plus the possibility of under-saddle suspension. All other considerations regarding cycle type are unimportant if any of the above are not set right for **you**. Correct frame size and saddle design and height are probably the two most important factors. Look

Looking North near Little Asby

closely to the three areas where you are in contact with your cycle: backside, hands and feet.

CYCLE HIRE

Not everyone owns a cycle and so, other than borrowing one, cycle hire is the only alternative. Details of Cycle Hire locations in Cumbria can be found on www.lakedistrictoutdoors.com. If borrowing a cycle is the chosen option, please ensure it is the right size, well maintained and in good condition. Whether borrowing or hiring, take time to be certain you have the correct size and fit – see previous section for what to look for.

ACCESSORIES

There is not a lot of equipment that can be carried on a cycle so what is carried needs to be well thought out. **Panniers** are often deemed to be specialist items not owned by most casual cyclists but for cycle touring they are the best option. Buy the best you can afford and ideally choose ones which are 100% waterproof and hard wearing. Attach a pannier frame to your bike and leave it on all year as it is really useful without being a nuisance. The larger **rear panniers** are more expensive and ideal for longer expeditions but resist the temptation to overfill. In preference, choose a pair of front wheel

panniers and use them on the rear for most week-long trips. If you need more space then you need more experience to help you select what you need to take and what you don't! Add a lightweight waterproof roll-top bag to complete the set which can be bungeed lengthwise on the top of the pannier frame when in use. Store it rolled up no more than the size of (and lighter than) a small newspaper. In any event, include a couple of bungees to strap your discarded clothing onto your pannier frame when you start to overheat.

A **handlebar bag** is a very useful extra to carry your personal essentials (including a Swiss Army knife complete with scissors), always in view and easily taken off by you at every parking situation and carried in hand or as a small shoulder bag. This way it is never out of your sight. The flat top is ideal for positioning a press stud attached map case and reading the contents as you cycle. NB This guide is designed to fit into such an accessory. With practice you can learn to fold an OS map so that you can follow a visible route which continues on the other side of the map fold by turning over the map case (and therefore the map) and relocating it on top of the bar bag without having to remove the map from the map case. Not a lot of people know this!

Saddle bags work well but are not so popular these days. An option is a rear 'bag on a bar' clamped onto your seat stem for short trips with minimal luggage. Other than in winter for additional clothing and spare food, do not consider carrying a rucksack. Waist-belt bumbags have their uses but are generally not advisable during the summer months as they induce sweat and negate 'wicking'.

Most bike frames offer the possibility of carrying two **water bottles**. One is essential but a second is a preference. Always opt for the large size of bottle, i.e. one litre, and choose a clear colour so that the contents (both planned and unplanned) can be seen at a glance. Always thoroughly clean at the end of each day and replace at frequent intervals. The other option is a backpack water bag with a drinking tube attached – superb on hot days but must be kept clean.

Attaching a **small triangle bag** in the corner of the bike frame provides handy storage space for a basic first aid kit plus one or two very useful tools. A *basic first aid kit* should contain: 2 x crepe bandages, 1 x large Melolin dressing pad, 6 large safety pins (to make slings from pinned-up clothing), 6 antiseptic wipes, various sizes of elastoplast, 1 tube of antihistamine cream or tea-tree oil (for stings), 1 tube of suncream, 1 tube of midge cream (optional).

Handy tools could include a multi-tool set of Allen keys plus both types of screwdriver, an electrician's thin screwdriver and a tyre lever, all of which are best kept quickly to hand.

A **wedge saddle bag** is another piece of useful equipment to carry items which may be called upon from time to time, e.g. spare inner tube, puncture repair kit, roll of electrician's tape, small adjustable spanner, chain splitter, pair of surgical gloves (for chain work), tube of oil removal cream, emergency Mars bar and a strong polythene carrier bag (many uses including a temporary repair lining for a split tyre wall). Take a small bag of nuts and bolts plus some strong wire to effect emergency repairs. Some cyclists like to pack in a very thin windproof/showerproof top as an extra layer for those unexpected weather changes.

A good quality **lock** is recommended but make sure you have the key with you before closing and check this on each and every occasion. It is wise to carry the key on a cord which you can wear around your neck whilst your cycle is locked. Both cord and key can be carried in the triangle bag at other times. A strong lock attached to a long section of strengthened plastic-coated cable can be fed through your seat support and kept there permanently, tucked below your seat so it is never forgotten, and can be threaded around a hooped stand or a fixed object in a trice. Remember to include your frame in this process to avoid having your bike stolen with the exception of the saddle! Standing three bikes side by side and head to toe with the pedals vertical to keep the bikes close together will allow you to lock all three cycles to one another and, possibly, a fixed object if space permits.

There are a number of small accessories with various degrees of usefulness. A decent *bicycle pump* is a must and should be securely attached to your cycle. A dual valve fitting is a bonus. The law says your cycle should have a *bell* fitted at point of sale and its timely use to warn others of your approach does no harm and a lot of good. *Odometers* can provide some interesting information but are prone to failure on rough terrain. *Bar extensions* for mountain bikes and hybrids are popular as they provide a change of hand position, the best design being short with a bend and attached at a flat angle. This means they do not cause chest injury IF an over-the-handlebars manoeuvre is attempted at exceedingly short notice. Thick foam padding around the main grip and extensions is recommended for comfort and warmth in colder weather.

CLOTHING

The weather obviously has a bearing on what clothing is suitable. But, whatever the weather and whatever the time of year, good quality **padded shorts** are the priority consideration. This really is a bum decision so get it right and feel the benefits!

Even in hot weather, **padded gloves** are worth wearing for comfort and, just in case of a fall, in order to protect vulnerable palms. The style with an Aertex reverse side are cool to wear but have poor absorption qualities when you need them. Fleece gloves with reinforced palms are fine for colder days whilst medium weight ski-style gloves are best for the real winter months. Waterproof gloves are a matter of preference but not universally liked perhaps due to the tight fit and 'sweaty palms' factor.

Choice of **footwear** depends on choice of pedals. Clip-on pedals require clip-in shoes of which there is a wide selection but the waterproof variety are recommended for winter wear. Touring cyclists and those preferring flexibility who choose 'clip-on' pedals (SPDs) should consider reversible pedals which have one clip-on side and one normal flat pedal. Toe clips are the alternative option if you are keen to include an upward pull as you pedal. For those who prefer to cycle without either then make sure your footwear supports your foot properly and has a firm base to prevent foot fatigue and bruising. Always ensure the ball of the foot is pressing on the pedal (see saddle height recommendations) and tuck your lace loops into your lace crossovers to avoid catching them on the chain.

As for **helmets**, as ever the choice is yours but make sure you understand all the issues. Cycling is good for your health. Not cycling is probably more dangerous for your health. Head injuries, however caused and however unlikely, never bring happiness and if wearing a good quality, ventilated and properly fitting helmet reduces the chances of head injury from the many unforeseen circumstances for which they have been designed then that can only be of positive benefit. Having witnessed the trauma that always comes with head injury, this writer always wears a helmet with visor but believes in individual choice. Non helmet wearers should use a well-fitting peak cap to avoid sunburn.

Go for lightweight layers but make sure they are all made from wicking fabrics (which have the ability to move sweat from the body to the atmosphere and dry quickly when wet). Some makes don't smell even if sweated in and, being quick drying, can be washed each night. Forget cotton tee shirts, rugby tops and the like – they are barrier garments which act as blotting paper with little practical use on a cycle tour.

Hot/warm dry days: socks, shorts and wicking tee-shirt (such as coolmax) + lightweight breathable shirt-type top.

Cool dry/showery days: the above plus a fleece type top and a lightweight windproof/showerproof top.

Cold dry/wet days: the above plus stretch pants (windproof/quick drying) plus a good quality 'breathable' waterproof jacket. (There are about 30 different makes of breathable fabrics to choose from, some better than others and that includes several minority makes. Look for the fabric's ability to 'breathe', its recovery time when totally soaked and comfort when dry or wet. Remember – biggest isn't always best!)

These are guidelines but it is time-gained experience of what works and what doesn't which will guide your clothing choices. There are numerous specialist manufacturers of cyclist clothing who make first-class products but good quality outdoor activity clothing is every bit as reliable. Whatever your preference make sure you choose a bright colour for your safety, to help ensure other road users see you and for good photographs!

SUN PROTECTION

Sunburn occurs on hot sunny days but can also happen when it is cloudy as the sun's UV rays penetrate the cloud. This is not always obvious particularly if there's a wind which is keeping you cool while you burn. Windburn can also damage the skin. You must protect against both by regular application of a suitably strong suncream and don't forget to use lip protection and/or lip salve to counteract dried-out lips which can be painful. Some parts of the body are more vulnerable than others when cycling including foreheads, the back of the neck, ears, upper arms, thighs and calves. Cycling the PCW from south to north will expose the right side of your body to the sun and the back of your body in the afternoons. Be aware of this and either wear long sleeves and a neckerchief or keep topping up the cream on all those body parts facing the sun even if *you* are not. Don't take your skin for granted and the same goes for your eyes which should be protected by decent sunglasses on sunny days and lightweight clear glasses (try your builder's merchant shop) on wet or dull days. Hitting a bluebottle flying at 30mph can spoil everyone's holiday!

FOOD AND DRINK

Food is your body's energy supply and an appropriate drink the lubricant which keeps the moving parts working. Start each day with a good breakfast – larger than you would usually eat as you will be doing more exercise than you usually do. Eat little and often and avoid big meals during the ride. There is no substitute for pastas and rice which are both high in carbohydrates and allow the steady flow of energy during the post-digestion period. Highly seasoned food may cause rumblings (or worse) during subsequent cycling. Red meat eaten mid-ride can take a long time to digest and even longer

to provide energy to your muscles. As ever, fresh vegetables are good for you, especially broccoli, as is fresh fruit, particularly bananas. Carry a supply of energy nibbles with you including bananas, chocolate and energy bars. Make up your own 'energy bag' with a mixture of raisins, dried apricots (not too many) and your favourite dried sweet bites from health food shops. Save for those energy-drained moments and share with your companions to provide that all-important pick-me-up when it is needed most.

Energy drinks are a matter of choice but nothing takes the place of good clean water which your body needs in copious amounts during and after exercise. Drink often and frequently which is six times as much as 'once in a while'. Don't wait until you are thirsty as then it is too late. Remember that coffee, tea and alcohol actually *cause* dehydration but there is no need to avoid these drinks during a cycling trip if you prefer not to. The answer is to take them in moderation and always precede with up to a litre of water after moderate exercise and up to two or three litres after strenuous exercise, especially in hot weather. The rule is 'sip as you cycle' whether from your water bottle or backpack water bag of which there are several types on the market. And don't be too shy to ask for an en-route top up if you have drunk what you are carrying. Finally, during the evening begin your post-ride relaxation with a litre of water with or without cordial. You need to drink a minimum of five to six litres of water during each cycle day and more if it is hot. Not doing so will inevitably bring on gradual dehydration – its signs are: infrequent to nil toilet stops, strong yellow urine when you do go and headaches and constipation, all of which are avoidable and none of which you want at any time never mind whilst on holiday.

FINAL CONSIDERATIONS

You have discovered the PCW, read about the route, learned the necessary lessons, made your decisions and laid your plans: all that is left to do now is do it. So book the dates and make it happen. You won't regret it and, when you get back, you can start the whole process over again with *another* route. Life might never be the same again!

Ford at Crosby Garrett

OS MAPS: Landranger 91 and 97
SUSTRANS MAP: PCW (NCN Route 68 Derby–Appleby)

The Pennine Cycleway takes you on a magnificent journey through the fells of upland Britain and nothing short of stunning and ever-changing scenery provides the setting and backdrop for the first day of this memorable cycle tour.

The ride between Kendal and Appleby begins with lowly Lambrigg Fell then passes the loftier Howgills, with the fells of distant Lakeland to the west and the Pennines to the north. On a clear day, wonderful views turn into stunning vistas.

The Lune Gorge and the Howgills

Stage 1
KENDAL TO APPLEBY
63KM / 38 MILES

ROUTE POINTS

- Minor country roads and quiet lanes provide the route and yes there are hills but somehow, when done south to north, most of them seem to gain height gradually and descend at length.

- In the Lune gorge the **PCW** follows a Roman road, now little more than a 3m wide tarmac lane, probably built on the line of an even older trackway. This section provides something of a contrast in that the **PCW** briefly shares the same valley as the mainline rail and the M6 but you can cycle along the opposite hillside as if in another world. The motorway and railway are crossed three times then never seen again for the remainder of the journey.

- Orton is the start of limestone country with its rolling moors which change ever so gently into peaceful pastures and quiet meadows. Orton, Great Asby and Rutter Force provide rest stops – the first a lovely self-sufficient village with a variety of services, the second a very attractive sleepy village with one pub and the third a real gem of a place with a cafe and art centre by a superb waterfall. The small and attractive town of Appleby is a positive metropolis by comparison with a range of services – a worthy place to end the first stage of the **PCW**.

KENDAL

Kendal is known as the southern gateway to the Lake District but, looking eastward, it is also a doorway to the Yorkshire Dales, a threshold to the Howgill Fells and a doorstep to the Pennines. It is a fitting start to the northern half of the PCW and an equally fitting finish to the PCW (South). The West Coast mainline railway stops at out-of-town Oxenholme station and the A590(T) links easily with the M6 motorway 6 miles to the south. A visionary 'Park and Ride' scheme is envisaged for the future which would further enhance the choice of Kendal as the midpoint for the PCW for those preferring to complete the entire route over two separate weeks. Kendal is also the junction of several NCN CRs and at least two planned or amended regional long distance CRs. the town also makes a fine base for cycling – the easily accessible surrounding countryside in which the town nestles offering a wide range of CR choices to suit all tastes and abilities.

KENDAL TIC Tel: 01539 725758
Town Hall, Highgate, LA9 4DL
email kendaltic@southlakeland.gov.uk
CYCLE SHOPS & HIRE Bruces Cycle Shop, Tel: 01539 727230; Askews Cycle Shop, Tel: 01539 728057
LOOS AND BREWS aplenty
ACCOMMODATION Full range of hotels and B&Bs; Kendal YH, Tel: 0870 7705892
PUBLIC TRANSPORT West Coast mainline rail service to Oxenholme The Lake District enquiries, Tel: 08457 484950
VISITOR ATTRACTIONS The Brewery Arts Centre, Kendal Castle, Kendal Museums, Kays Shoe Factory
POINTS OF INTEREST A busy town full of historical interest and always full of hustle and bustle with major long term plans to re-open the Lancaster to Kendal Canal.

Kendal lies in a large basin sheltered by steep hills to the east along which lies the route of the PCW. Kendal-bound cyclists arriving from the north and south can freewheel steeply down and directly into the town but it makes sense for north- and south-bound cyclists to take the very pleasant and gently ascending longer route to reach the same point. This route also allows easy access to out-of-town Oxenholme railway station for cyclists travelling to / from the route via the main West Coast railway.

The northern section of the Pennine Cycleway starts in the town centre at the River Kent where you join the southbound traffic-free Canal Cycle Route paralleling the rather busy main road. *NB The Kendal & Lancaster Canal has long since been emptied but there are plans to reopen it.* This is NCN Route 6 which links Kendal with Lancashire. Follow this from the town centre [4km] as far as Natland, a small village with a corner shop for those last minute supplies. TL then keeping the church (L), pass under a railway bridge before carefully crossing the A65(T) [800m]. The Helm rises steeply (R) but the narrow lane ascends gently to cross the B6254 at the Railway Inn [1.6km]. Oxenholme station is 500m down to the left and makes for a short sharp climb up – at least from a standing start following a sitting journey!

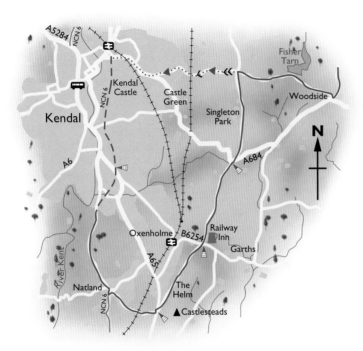

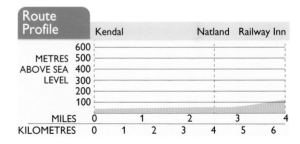

TIP OF THE DAY Before setting off each day, do get into the habit of checking your bike – wheels locked in, brakes working, chain lubed, sprockets and moving parts oiled, both gear tension jockey wheels de-gunged, everything attached that should be with no loose ends, water bottle(s) filled, zips zipped and laces tied so they won't catch

Route Profile	Kendal			Natland	Railway Inn

| METRES ABOVE SEA LEVEL | 600 500 400 300 200 100 | | | | |

| MILES | 0 | 1 | 2 | 3 | 4 |
| KILOMETRES | 0 | 1 | 2 | 3 | 4 | 5 | 6 |

Leaving/passing the PH behind you (R), continue north-east to cross the A684 [1.4km] then TR [1.6km] at the X-rds. **Note: Down L (west) is the quick way down to Kendal.** Climb gently past the mast (L) and Fisher Tarn behind the dam wall (L) to the next T-j [1.4km] then TL just before the A684. TL at the next T-j [1.2km] then a short downhill to TR [500m] to T-j just past Kiln Head Farm [2km]. TR to cross the M6 motorway [2km] then TL down to the offset X-rds at Beckfoot [1.5km].

Note: This road was formerly known as Old Scotch Road, the old drove road used for driving cattle south from Scotland by way of the Solway Estuary. Pause for a moment to take in the majestic sweep of the magnificent Lowgill Viaduct constructed as part of the Sedbergh–Kirkby Lonsdale–Clapham rail link closed in 1966.

TR then immediately TL under the viaduct to descend steeply to cross the River Lune by the old narrow bridge. You then begin the 'climb of the day' (DAP) up past the entrance to the aptly named Crook of Lune Farm to the T-j at Howgill [1.5km]. TL along the Roman road passing Gibbet Hill – a lovely spot to stop for a picnic. Continue to the quiet A685 beyond Low Borrowbridge Farm (*note: site of Roman fort*) passing under the M6 and the mainline railway [6.2km]. From here it is only 9km to rest and refreshments in the village of Orton!

TIP OF THE DAY   When coming to a stop in a high gear after a fast section – as you slow to a halt, change down several gears so that you are in the right gear for starting off again

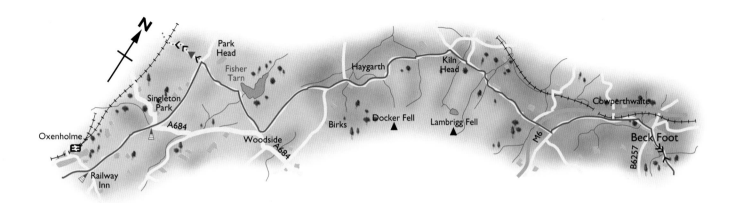

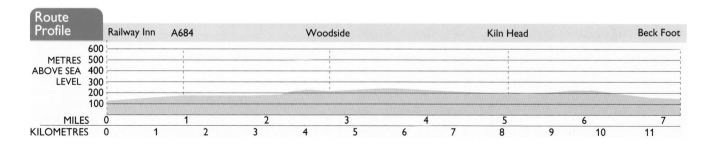

Rutter Force

TR along the relatively quiet A685 then TL [1km] onto the next minor road before crossing the river. After crossing Roundthwaite Beck, climb Loups Fell (DAP or 7 mins to cycle) and enjoy the well-earned descent to Greenholme Farm [3.2km] then SA along the very pleasant narrow lane which runs close to the picturesque Birk Beck as far as Scout Green [1.9km]. Ascend a short sharp 'slopelet' to re-pass under the mainline railway and the M6 for the last time. After Sproat Ghyll Farm (L) cruise down to Orton for a well-deserved rest and welcome refreshment.

Kendal to Orton: 40km (24 miles)

ORTON

Shop and PO (Cycle Hire)
Tearoom
Chocolate factory and tearoom
Kings Head PH

THE LUNE VALLEY

Cutting through the valley floor is the unspoilt River Lune, unsullied by the functional 'conduits' close by and above. There is the M6 motorway, the West Coast mainline railway, the old main road to Kendal, a power supply, a disused railway and a walking route. There is even the odd low-flying jet to view. The PCW also utilises this narrow corridor and, amazingly, it is not compromised or demeaned by living cheek by jowl with the above.

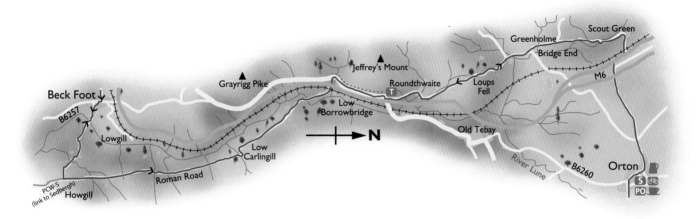

Scout Green
Greenholme
Bridge End
M6
Jeffrey's Mount
Roundthwaite
Loups Fell
Grayrigg Pike
Low Borrowbridge
Old Tebay
Beck Foot
B6257
Lowgill
Low Carlingill
River Lune
B6260
Orton
Roman Road
PCW-S (link to Sedbergh)
Howgill

N

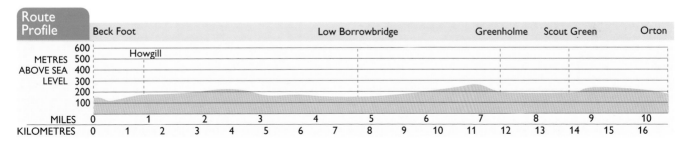

Route Profile

	Beck Foot	Low Borrowbridge	Greenholme	Scout Green	Orton

METRES ABOVE SEA LEVEL: 600 500 400 300 200 100

Howgill

MILES: 0 1 2 3 4 5 6 7 8 9 10
KILOMETRES: 0 1 2 3 4 5 6 7 8 9 10 11 12 13 14 15 16

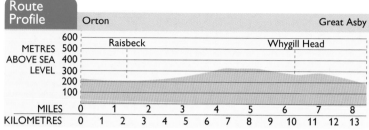

Route Profile — Orton — Great Asby

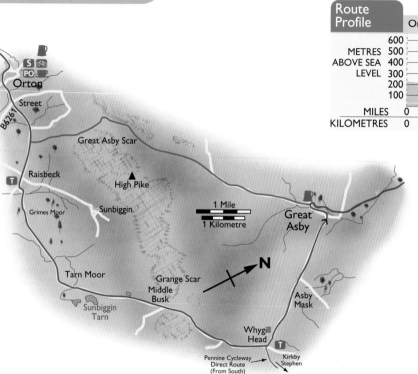

Great Asby Scar

Raisbeck

High Pike

Grimes Moor

Sunbiggin

1 Mile

1 Kilometre

Great Asby

Tarn Moor

Grange Scar
Middle Busk

Sunbiggin Tarn

Asby Mask

N

Whygill Head

Kirkby Stephen

Pennine Cycleway
Direct Route
(From South)

Orton

Street

B6261

Orton to Appleby is a very pleasant section of route which is much less demanding than anything so far experienced. The character of the scenery changes quite definitely as more and more limestone pavements, complete with criss-crossing clints and grykes, protrude out of the rolling moorland. The unfenced road offers fine views of Sunbiggin Tarn which is rich in wildlife. Great Asby is a sleepy gem of Cotswoldian-style charm and Rutter Force an unexpected delight. The unavoidable B6260 provides a less than satisfactory entry into Appleby but one which is more than compensated for by the pleasure of arrival.

On leaving Orton, keep the Kings Head PH (R) then TL along the quiet B6261 to the X-rds [600m]. SA to and through Raisbeck [1.5km] after which TL onto a slightly smaller road which crosses Tarn Moor to the X-rds at Whygill Head [8km]. TL to ascend only a little before the exhilarating descent to Great Asby [3.5km]. TL into the village – don't be tempted to bear R and so miss this lovely little village. TR across the stream at the church to rejoin the original road at the fork [1km]. Fork R then after 2km TL down to Rutter Force for refreshments as well as ducks and wasps on hot summer days! Cycle across the ford at your peril! Return to the route [250m] then TL to the next T-j [1km]. TL to Burrells where you TR onto the B6260 past the delightfully named Slosh Farm to the outskirts of Appleby. Either fork L along Doomsgate and after 300m TR to enter Appleby centre by Low Wiend (DAP) or alternatively SA up to Appleby Castle (be alert to traffic flow) and then down to the centre of the town.

Orton to Appleby: 23km (14miles)
TOTAL distance: 63km (38 miles)

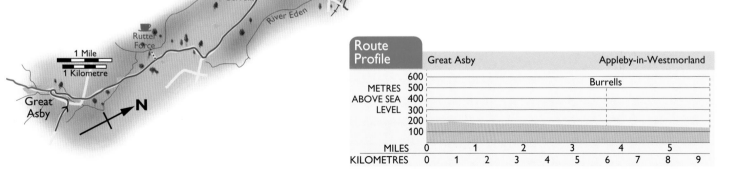

35

Kendal · Orton · Haltwhistle · Norham · Alston · Appleby · Bellingham · Wooler · Berwick-upon-Tweed · Rothbury

OS MAPS: Landranger 86 and 91
SUSTRANS MAP: PCW (NCN Route 68 Appleby–Berwick upon Tweed)

Today's route provides another memorable cycle journey. The first 23 miles along the highly scenic 'balcony road' and the quiet lanes between Hilton and Renwick give superb views of the lush Eden Valley with the Lake District beyond. This is followed by a climb up Hartside – either on- or off-road depending on preference – and then a welcome descent into England's highest market town, Alston. The onward sometimes hilly route down the picturesque South Tyne Valley is also braided, both strands of which provide fine views of the magnificent Lambley Viaduct before joining the traffic-free Haltwhistle Greenway down to the town itself.

A challenging day for many and tough for some but the day-long payback levels are at a constant high.

The Eden Valley from Hartside

ROUTE POINTS

- Today's recommended mileage is greater and more challenging than Day 1. It is, of course, possible to opt for shorter legs – a stay overnight in Alston would allow Haltwhistle to be reached by noon the following day with ample time to cycle along the impressive Lambley Viaduct. **NB** It is possible to cycle onto the viaduct but not completely over it as the vital last section of DRT on the south side is in private ownership – access is from/to the northern end but well worth the short diversion.

- The anaerobic ascent of Hartside shares the award-winning braided **C2C Cycle Route 7** which offers a partly off-road alternative or a tarmac option both of which are signed. The descent to Alston is a just reward. Alston is a popular overnight location for **C2C Cycle Route** cyclists so beds may be in demand at busy times.

- Today's route offers a fine opportunity to include the recommended half-day cycle tour to Hadrian's Wall as shown on page 53. Carvoran Roman Army Museum is well worth a visit and the recommended route a delight in its own right especially if the off-road version is chosen (suitable for all cycles except those with narrow racing tyres).

APPLEBY

Appleby lies on the banks of the River Eden only 4km below the fells of the North Pennines. It is a quaint historical town famous for its annual horse fair which attracts participants and visitors from all over the world. Appleby Castle sits proudly above the town's main tree-lined avenue. Street names like Doomgate and Low Wiend only hint at Appleby's rich past. The town is served by the famous Carlisle to Settle railway line which continues to thrive due to a combination of popular demand and pride. Each train has space for up to six cycles if neatly stacked but this author has often seen a few more squeezed in, such is the level of customer care offered. Appleby is also the junction with a second CR which is NCN Route 67 between Penrith and the Vale of York. The PCW shares the alignment of Regional Route 20 between Barrow in Furness and Sunderland as far as Kirkby Stephen via Whygill Head X-rds. Appleby also makes a good short-break base for cycle touring.

APPLEBY TIC Moot Hall, Boroughgate, CA16 6XE. Tel: 017683 51177, email tic@applebytown.org.uk
CYCLE SHOP Nearest hire, spares and repairs is in Kirkby Stephen Cycle Centre, Tel: 017683 71658/72442, www.kirkbystephencyclecentre.com
LOOS AND BREWS Choice of tearooms, toilets and general supplies
ACCOMMODATION Hotels and B&Bs; nearest YH at Dufton, Tel 0870 770 5800 email dufton@yha.org.uk
PUBLIC TRANSPORT Regional Railways' Carlisle to Settle and Leeds line, enquiries Tel: 08457 484950
VISITOR ATTRACTIONS Appleby Castle, Appleby Horse Fair in June
POINTS OF INTEREST The beautiful church of St Laurence, peaceful court-yard of St Annes's Hospital, Appleby Grammar School attended by the half brothers of George Washington.

Cross the River Eden by the main bridge and TR (take care) to head south-west for 400m then TL to ascend under the Carlisle to Settle railway line. TR alongside a once-thriving dairy produce factory. At the next T-j, TL to soon pass under the always busy A66(T) then TR leaving the town of Appleby behind [1km]. The unfolding route ahead climbs gently and easily up to the small settlement of Hilton [4km] paralleling Hilton Beck and taking advantage of the same topography. *Naming this part of the route the 'balcony road' is the author's idea, so-called because it contours the Eden Valley for many miles and, in the tradition of the very best high balconies, offers an amazing yet constantly changing vista with the picturesque Eden Valley in the foreground and the ever beautiful Lake District in the distance.*

TL at Hilton through Murton and cycle easily to a point where it is possible to freewheel to the outskirts of Dufton. Take time to look westward to appreciate the view.

Dufton is a lovely village with broad tree-lined greens. It has an old pub offering food and accommodation although at the time of going to press the old style Youth Hostel is barely surviving the post foot and mouth period due to reduced numbers of Pennine Way walkers and short break clientèle. Hopefully PCW cyclists will help to ensure its continued life of service to Pennine journey folk whatever their favoured mode of transport.

From the River Eden, the PCW is also signed via/from the railway station but the route shown in this guide avoids the steep hill up to the station.

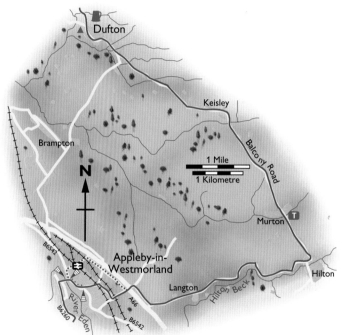

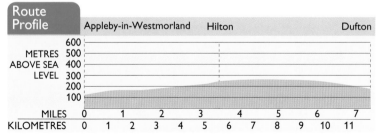

Route Profile

	Appleby-in-Westmorland	Hilton		Dufton

METRES ABOVE SEA LEVEL	600 500 400 300 200 100

MILES	0	1	2	3	4	5	6	7
KILOMETRES	0	1 2	3	4	5 6	7	8 9	10 11

CUMBRIA CYCLEWAY

The western section of the Cumbria Cycleway (CCW) also follows the alignment of the PCW between Kirkby Stephen and Renwick. The CCW was the very first county circular cycle route to be promoted in the UK but some of the roads it originally used are no longer suitable for a promoted CR. Following a safety audit, it has been agreed to realign relevant sections of the CCW to co-incide with the NCN. The CCW no longer takes the direct route to/from Appleby but now follows the PCW as described and signed, though it should be said that should you be forced to **descend** directly from Dufton to Appleby for whatever reason, the route shown on the current OS Landranger series is acceptable as it takes full advantage of gravity.

HELM WIND

One less than pleasant feature of this part of the world – and fortunately one which happens only occasionally – is the 'Helm wind' which blows from the east. It is an extraordinarily strong wind which funnels over the top of the Pennines and directly down to the Vale of Eden through which the PCW passes. Though infrequent, the Helm wind is not to be taken lightly and your progress will be 100 per cent more enjoyable for its passing!

The 'balcony route' is characterised by a series of more or less equidistant farm communities, hamlets and villages, some of which offer accommodation though shops are few and far between. However, a number of quiet rural pubs exist along the route hanging onto life by their fingertips. The PCW continues northwards out of Dufton through Knock (meaning a hillock), then onto Milburn [6km] where you should TR to cycle by the long village green as opposed to taking the narrow lane 'bypass'.

Note: South-bound cyclists leaving Milburn and needing to reach Appleby in a hurry could take the almost direct road through Long Martin twice passing under the Carlisle to Settle railway line to reach Appleby quickly and enjoyably though the poorer experience-wise for missing out Knock, Dufton and Hilton.

Between Knock and Milburn there is only one TR after 4.5km. Blencarn is the next rural community [2.5km] which like Milburn, also has a small 'bypass' road which would miss out the village altogether. TR into Blencarn as your continuation route leaves the village at its north end. The short hill soon eases and Kirkland is then reached [1.5km]. TL and roll gently down to Skirwith [3km] to TR at the X-rds, then it's on to Ousby [2.5km]. *Note: The off-road option which links Kirkland more directly with Ousby. The PCW Route 68 signs should indicate a L fork just before Ousby and the*

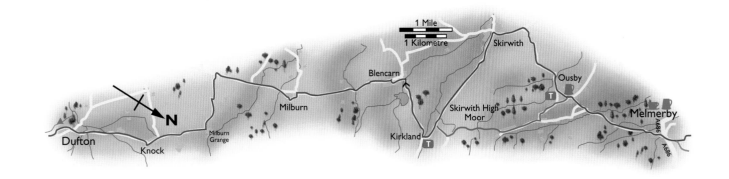

1 Mile

1 Kilometre

Skirwith

Blencarn

Ousby

Dufton

Knock

Milburn

Milburn
Grange

Skirwith High
Moor

Kirkland

Melmerby

A686

A686

N

Route Profile		Dufton	Knock			Milburn		Blencarn	Kirkland			Skirwith		Ousby	Melmerby

METRES ABOVE SEA LEVEL	600 500 400 300 200 100

MILES	0	1	2	3	4	5	6	7	8	9	10	11
KILOMETRES	0 1	2	3 4	5	6 7	8	9 10	11 12	13 14	15	16 17	

MELMERBY

Melmerby is the largest and busiest village since Dufton with several B&Bs, an excellent pub serving very good value meals and a home bakery tearoom which sells tasty if rather expensive food produced from organic flour. The A686 linking Penrith with the Tyne Valley via Hartside passes through Melmerby. Recently voted by the AA as one the world's top 10 motoring drives, this road is hugely popular with motorbikers at weekends who travel many miles to race their machines up and down Hartside. Originally engineered by John Loudon McAdam in 1823/24, the A686 boasts an almost completely even gradient throughout its length, the many switchbacks providing entertainment for the motorbikers who, it has to be said, do tend to treat cyclists with respect.

ALSTON

Alston is an attractive high Pennines town with steep cobbled streets and a distinct aura of 'time has passed us by'. It has been the setting for several films and TV dramas. It is an interesting little town and well worth taking time to replenish your supplies. Just up and around the corner from the TIC, there is a very good cafe/tearoom adjacent to an outdoor shop both of which are well known for service and value for money. The narrow gauge railway, with yet another tearoom, is well worth visiting as is the unsophisticated Hub transport museum.

TR after 400m to gently undulate to Melmerby [2km] being 30km (18 miles) from Appleby.

Though the PCW only briefly follows the A686, vigilance is recommended. Keep SA to cruise to and through the delightful unspoilt village of Gamblesby [2km]. *The recommended off-road option which forks right just 300m beyond Melmerby misses the village although a connecting spur does exist.* 1km after Gamblesby TL before taking the Unthank 'bypass' to roll along to Busk 5 Lane Ends (a further 2km). Here the C2C Route 7 meets the PCW Route 68. TR up the track to follow the off-road option – continue SA to drop down quite steeply to join the on-road CR which climbs (and climbs) up to the summit of Hartside (DAP) with its cafe and fine views. NB South-bound cyclists should take the longer route shown on the map to avoid the steep and badly sighted uphill section to Busk 5 Lane Ends.

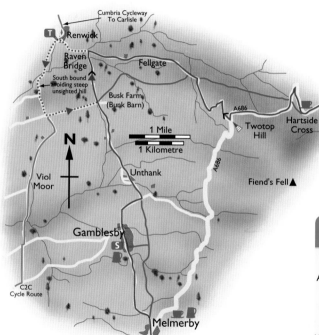

CARLISLE LINK

The CCW continues up the western flank of the last section of the true North Pennines to Castle Carrock, a small but pleasant village a little south of Brampton. Here the route interconnects with NCN Route 72 which is set to become Hadrian's Cycleway when fully open – hopefully by 2005. This CR follows the entire length of the Hadrian's Wall World Heritage Site corridor between Ravenglass on the west coast of Cumbria and the mouth of the River Tyne via Carlisle. The Tyne Valley railway passes close to Brampton and carries a minimum of two cycles but often one or two more depending on space and demand. To cycle to Carlisle, which is on the West Coast mainline railway, TL at or before Castle Carrock and follow NCN Route 72 signs to the city.

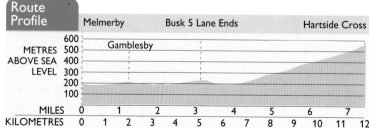

Renwick to Hartside is always a memorable experience no matter how often you do it. The height difference is 500m over the on-road 6km and the same over the off-road 4.5km. Once the A686 is reached then be prepared to be passed by more than just the odd motorbike. The cafe at the summit of Hartside is the meeting point for motor-bikers and cyclists although the latter earn their rest stop with more sweat and sometimes a few tears! The ensuing downhill is a welcome change provided you have not chosen a day when there is a 'beastly easterly'. After 5km, TR down steeply to the Leadgate T-j where the main C2C route departs R (south). Alston is not far so TL and follow the C2C short-cut option to rejoin the A686 for 400m and the run into Alston.

Appleby to Alston: 55km (33 miles)

Leave Alston on the A686 for 1km then SA along the minor road which leads to Randalholme (possibly meaning an isolated strip of unploughed land in a valley) after which the road reduces to a most pleasing narrow lane close to the River South Tyne. Pass the eye-catching Kirkhaugh Church with its needle-like spire then change down the gears to cycle (or DAP) up the shortish but very steep hill to Low Row. TL along yet another balcony road past a recently closed primitive drift mine (R) and Baraugh Hall (L: pronounced Baruff) before descending carefully to a ford followed by an extremely steep S bend (DAP). Continue most pleasantly to

cross the River Tyne and join the A689 for 600m (take care) to TL into the delightfully named village of Slaggyford [1km].

Pass the village green and TR up to the old station house then TR pleasantly along the DRT until the A689 is crossed by means of the Burnstone Viaduct. After 50m TL onto the A689; TL under the skewed-arched viaduct then TL off the main road to Knarsdale church (PH 200m R). TL and down to cross the R South Tyne and along to the Eals T-j where you can glimpse the ancient field system still in use. TR and begin the last ascent of the day if finishing at Haltwhistle (133m over 2km) followed by a steady descent to Lanehead X rds.

For Lambley Viaduct TL down to Coanwood and TL at the houses, gently down to access the DRT at a double set of gates. TL and cycle easily along to the viaduct [4km there and back]. This hugely impressive viaduct was built to carry the Alston railway line over the South Tyne river before it was closed in 1974. Though not part of a through route, the viaduct was opened for public access after major renovation in 1999. Don't miss it!

From the much smaller but skillfully built Burnstones Viaduct, the off-road option continues along the DRT to Railway Cottages [4.5km] from where there is a fine view of Lambley Viaduct. This route really is recommended to off-road cyclists for the views, the

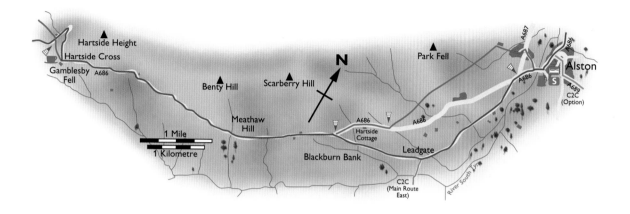

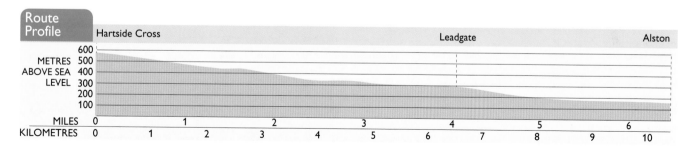

special nature of the track and to avoid the steep road route! Until planned improvements have been completed, the surface is mixed and less enjoyable after a long spell of wet weather. TL up a short but very steep tarmac road (DAP) with superb views of the viaduct to reach the A689 [400m]. TR and cycle with care to the 2nd TR [500m] to descend to cross the River South Tyne. The ensuing ascent up to where the DRT crosses the road is not particularly arduous. It is well signed but the gate (R) which leads to the viaduct [4km there and back] is rather innocuous – see Lambley Viaduct info. On returning from the viaduct, recross the road and continue very pleasantly to rejoin the main route at the disused Featherstone station below Rowfoot. *Note: PH nearby.*

During World War 2, the riverside area below Featherstone Castle was a POW camp whose occupants worked on local farms, some of whom stayed after the war and married locally. At one point, the Alston Railway was used to 'hide' the Royal Train during the war.

Road cyclists will need to retrace their wheels back up to Lanehead X-rds then TL to Rowfoot. TL down to the privately owned Featherstone station platform on your R shortly after the PH (L). TR at the old platform for the most enjoyable traffic-free run down into Haltwhistle [5km] though the A69(T) crossing needs great care. One further option is to continue down past Featherstone Castle, a part of which is now a rather basic bunkhouse, then very scenically

along the river to climb back up to the top road. TR to join the Haltwhistle Greenway. *Note: The author recommended to Sustrans the acquisition of this section of DRT and takes great pleasure from seeing the enjoyment it now brings to local people and visitors alike.* Though non-formalised, local people seem to have tacit permission from the landowner to pass under the A69(T) next to the South Tyne by means of the concrete road adjacent to the trunk road. A continuation track passes under Alston Arches, another impressive viaduct once used by the Alston Railway to connect with the minor road the other side of the A69(T). Hopefully this much safer and more practical route will become formalised in the fullness of time. Either way – Haltwhistle awaits!

Alston to Haltwhistle: 26km (15.5 miles)
Distance from Appleby: 80km (48 miles)
TOTAL distance from Kendal: 143km (86 miles)

Lambley viaduct

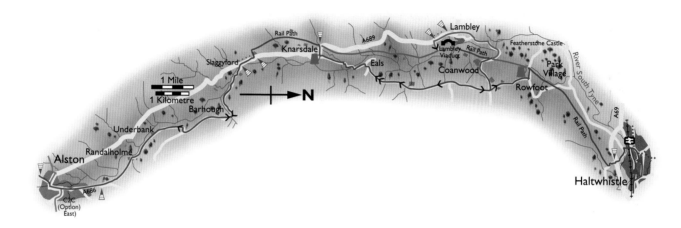

Lambley
Rail Path
A689
Knarsdale
Featherstone Castle
Lambley Viaduct
Rail Path
Eals
Rail Path
Coanwood
Park Village
Slaggyford
Rowfoot
River South Tyne
1 Mile
1 Kilometre
Barhough
N
A69
Underbank
Rail Path
Randalholme
Alston
Haltwhistle
A686
C2C (Option) East

Route Profile

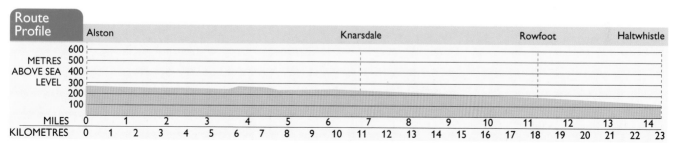

| | Alston | | | | | | | Knarsdale | | | | Rowfoot | | Haltwhistle |

| METRES ABOVE SEA LEVEL | 600 500 400 300 200 100 |

MILES: 0 1 2 3 4 5 6 7 8 9 10 11 12 13 14

KILOMETRES: 0 1 2 3 4 5 6 7 8 9 10 11 12 13 14 15 16 17 18 19 20 21 22 23

Kendal
Orton
Appleby
Alston
Haltwhistle
Bellingham
Rothbury
Wooler
Norham
Berwick-upon-Tweed

OS MAPS: Landranger 86 and 80
SUSTRANS MAP: PCW (NCN Route 68 Appleby–Berwick upon Tweed)

Haltwhistle in the upper reaches of the South Tyne valley is one of the principal 'gateway' towns for Hadrian's Wall behind which lies mile upon mile of wild, wonderful and virtually trackless countryside – an area of splendid isolation rich in history and wrapped in folklore. This is where the Northumberland National Park begins – England's most northern and least populated national park.

The route takes you past the Wall and into and through the Border Forest which boasts the biggest man-made lake in Europe set amidst the largest man-made forest in Europe – Kielder Water and Kielder Forest respectively.

Hadrian's Wall

HALTWHISTLE TO BELLINGHAM
46KM / 27 MILES

ROUTE POINTS

- Today's relatively short mileage is conditioned by two factors: firstly, the distance to the next community of any size after Bellingham and secondly, Hadrian's Wall which is unique and, being a World Heritage Site, should be enjoyed whilst the opportunity presents itself. In any event, visiting the Hadrian's Wall area by cycle is a special privilege and should be savoured not rushed.

- Whether or not it was possible to do the half day or evening cycle tour to Carvoran Roman Army Museum from Haltwhistle, do try to visit Vindolanda which is very close to the main route. NCN Route 72 (Hadrian's Cycleway) intersects with the PCW at this point and passes both of its entrances. Once Brewed Information Centre is also interesting and being en route is less time-consuming, whilst Steel Rigg provides one of the classic views of Hadrian's Wall.

- The road surface in the Border Forest Park is less than ideal due to the not infrequent passage of haulage transport.

- Stonehaugh offers basic services but soon the terrain softens as the route meanders and undulates down to the quiet valley of the North Tyne and the sleepy town of Bellingham.

HALTWHISTLE

Unusually named Haltwhistle* is a large, functional community which sees itself more like a very small town. Now bypassed by the A69(T), its useful range of shops and services will meet all your journeying needs. Haltwhistle's boast is that it is the geographical centre of Britain but it also lies close to the middle and best surviving section of Hadrian's Wall which can be readily accessed by cycle from Haltwhistle. The scenic Newcastle to Carlisle regional railway stops at Haltwhistle and the local TIC is situated at the station.

One theory is the name comes from 'halt' and 'twizell' meaning 'the place entwined between two rivers', in this case the River South Tyne and the Tippalt Burn.

NORTHUMBERLAND NATIONAL PARK AUTHORITY Tel: 01434 605555 admin@nnpa.org.uk

CYCLE HIRE/SPARES Eden's Lawn Garage, Haltwhistle, Tel: 01434 320443; limited spares also at Greggs Sports, Market Square, Haltwhistle, Tel: 01434 320255

HALTWHISTLE TIC is at the railway station, Tel: 01434 322002; regional railway and main bus route between Newcastle and Carlisle – see travel section for contact details

LOOS AND BREWS Tearooms, fish and chip shop, pizza takeaway; variety of shops; public toilets

VISITOR ATTRACTIONS Carvoran Roman Army Museum (see half day cycle tour) Tel: 016977 47485; Vindolanda Roman Museum and site of active archaeology (excavations) and interpretation centre, Tel: 01434 344277

UNLIKELY BUT TRUE There is a staircase in a building in Haltwhistle which is identical in every respect to the one in the Titanic – the 'unsinkable' ocean liner which sank in 1912 after hitting an iceberg.

The south/north PCW now shares the alignment of the west/east Hadrian's Cycleway (HCW) along the Tyne Valley as far as Bardon Mill (7km). *Note: This is NCN Route 72 which begins at Ravenglass on the west coast of Cumbria and runs through the full length of the Hadrian's Wall World Heritage Site corridor via Carlisle to the mouth of the River Tyne.* For the next 11km (6.6 miles), the CR signs now show route numbers 68 for the PCW and 72 for what will become the HCW when fully opened from end to end, hopefully by 2005. Until then, the 'open' sections can be cycled and enjoyed in their own right.

Haltwhistle on the South Tyne

TIP OF THE DAY Remember to ALWAYS check all the way round the inside of your tyre after puncturing in case a thorn or piece of glass remains embedded – remove from the outside with pliers if necessary

51

Exit Haltwhistle along the main street travelling east to drop down to the town's original bypass which is now a quiet, straight C road. NB. Enter Haltwhistle *from* the east by cycling along this C road then TR before Eden's Lawn garage (Cycle Hire). To continue the south/north route, TL under the A69(T). It is hard to believe but this road was the old A69; it runs between the railway on its low side (below which is the South Tyne) and the new trunk road on its upper side. Follow this lightly-trafficked now minor road along the Tyne Valley corridor to Bardon Mill (7km) first passing through Melkridge and then Redburn. *NB. On the other side of the now closely parallel A69(T) is Henshaw filling station and vehicle repair business which does emergency cycle repairs.* The road undulates into Bardon Mill (PH) now well known for its high quality kilns producing king-size glazed pots and chimneys (tearoom).

At Bardon Mill, TL under the A69(T) to begin the steady climb up to Hadrian's Wall. *Note: On both sides of the minor road opposite the TL, there are two fine examples of bastle houses – fortified farmhouses built to withstand the Border Reivers (see panel, page 78).*

The route is mostly uphill to Steel Rigg, which sits astride Hadrian's Wall (5km), but takes advantage of the least steep roads to a point where you can take an off-road short cut to Vindolanda (SA). The tarmac route continues more gently up to the T-j where the TR to follow NCN Route 72 (Hexham link) passes by both entrances to Vindolanda. The off-road short cut returns to the main route at this T-J. The Once Brewed Information Centre (machine refreshments) is soon reached where there is a YH and the Twice Brewed PH. *Note: So named because on an occasion long since past the beer was badly brewed and the local military ordered it to be brewed again.*

Be alert as you cross the straight and fast B6318, noticing the Vallum on either side. *Note: The Vallum was a deep ditch which paralleled the length of the Wall and was built by the Romans as yet a further line of defence along the bottom of which troops could move unseen. The B6318 is also known as the Military Road built by General Wade in the 1700s with large quantities of stone taken from the Roman Wall, its purpose being to move his army quickly across England's narrowest neck.*

TIP OF THE DAY   When cycling, the widest part of your foot should be positioned directly over the centre of the pedal with your upper body weight positioned centrally between the two wheels

Optional circuit to Hadrian's Wall and Carvoran Roman Army Museum

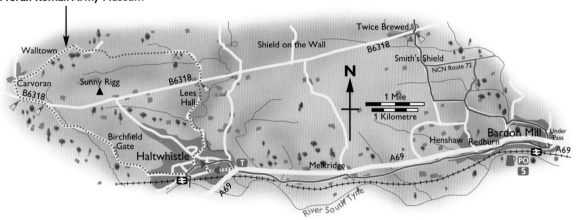

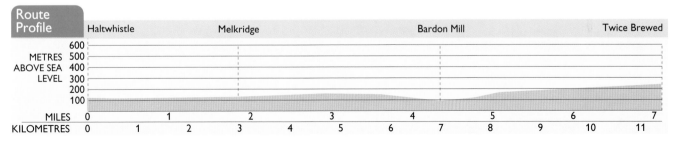

Climb up to Steel Rigg car park passing 'through' Hadrian's Wall to enjoy the view eastwards. Perhaps you will see some rock climbers on Peel Crag along which the Wall threads. *Note: Steel comes from 'stigol'(OE) meaning 'a way over a steep place' from which the word 'stile' is derived. Rigg is a corruption of 'ridge'.*

Tarry a while after Steel Rigg at the highest point to take in the view before you. Scotland lies in the distance yon side of the rolling Cheviot Hills. The Border Forest Park spreads its might in the middle distance beyond the Hadrian's Wall lakes (called 'loughs' – pronounced 'loffs') and huge expanses of rough upland pastures. Look north-eastwards and what you see is the journey ahead. If you can't see it then it must be bad weather and you should take this writer's word for it and press on in hope of a change for the better. Enjoy the descent that follows but take care!

TR to head north then wind pleasantly towards the forest along tiny roads which eventually peter out at the entrance to Scotchcoulthard (8km). *This is probably the place where 'Northumbrian' Reivers gathered up previously stolen horses or herds reclaimed from the Scottish side in the shelter of the ridge.* Beyond this ridge, the PCW then takes the unsurfaced unclassified road to Grindon Green (3km) now a cycle-friendly track through the forest. The continuation route is a wagon-width haulage road and none too smooth but it is the only through-route. Take care and grit your teeth for this section – literally – until you rejoin the tarmac at Whygate (4km) – pronounced Wiggit by the locals. This part of the route provides a bumpy ride for mountain bikes and hybrids but road cycles, other than those with narrow tyres, can manage with care.

Point of Interest: The Haining is a farm a little north of the unsurfaced road west of Whygate. 'To hain' is to enclose or preserve grass from being eaten by stock for a reason – for example, to turn it into hay. Originally, it meant an enclosure probably used to keep cattle in rather than out.

From here it is just 2km to the T-j to Stonehaugh – originally created as a Forestry Commission village but mechanisation has reduced

---

TIP OF THE DAY   Change gear just before and whilst going up hill or over tricky terrain – smoothly changing down consecutive gears whilst maintaining steady momentum even if slowing in the process

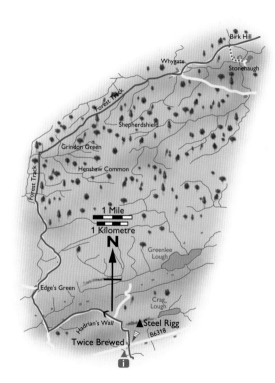

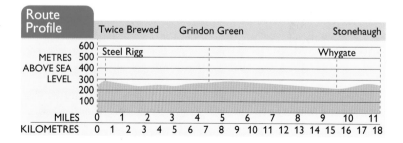

Route Profile			
Twice Brewed	Grindon Green		Stonehaugh
Steel Rigg			Whygate

| METRES ABOVE SEA LEVEL | 600 500 400 300 200 100 | | |

MILES 0 1 2 3 4 5 6 7 8 9 10 11

KILOMETRES 0 1 2 3 4 5 6 7 8 9 10 11 12 13 14 15 16 17 18

Forest cycle track to Grindon Green

manpower needs making it redundant for the purpose it was built. TR to divert into Stonehaugh (2 x 800m) to visit its public toilets, the campsite (with plans for a bunkbarn) or the local PH which serves drinks and refreshments at weekends and main holidays.

The forest is soon left behind but not the lumbering timber transporters with whom you will occasionally share the next 4km of route to Hetherington Farm (B&B). Cyclists are advised not to try and force these large vehicles off the road. *Note: There is an off-route bunkbarn/cottage nearby with basic facilities and plans for at least one further camping barn – check with Bellingham TIC for more details.* The remaining 8km to Bellingham feature changing views with several excellent en route viewpoints leading to a superb downhill to the intersection with the Reivers Cycle Route (RCR) numbered Regional Route 10. *Note: The RCR is another cycle route originated by this author from Tyneside via the Borderlands and Carlisle to Whitehaven (being the start of the C2C Cycle Route) on the West Cumbrian coast, a distance of 171 miles.* TR for the level run into Bellingham, the main village in the beautiful and unspoilt valley of the River North Tyne.

Haltwhistle to Bellingham: 46km (27 miles)
TOTAL distance from Kendal: 189km (113 miles)

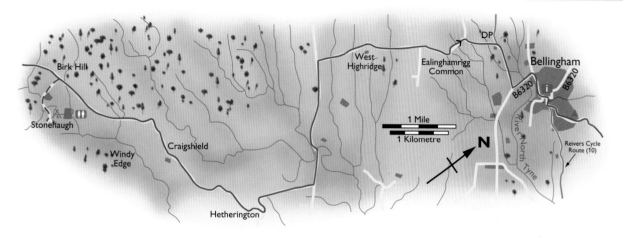

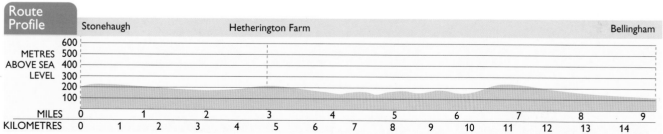

OS MAPS: Landranger 80 and 81
SUSTRANS MAP: PCW (NCN Route 68 Appleby–Berwick upon Tweed)

The PCW now takes on a different character with rolling heather-clad hills, bracken-strewn valleys and tree-lined streams. Big skies predominate. This is Northumberland at its most stunning – ever-changing with the seasons but with a timeless beauty. Though Cheviot itself is only 815m above sea level, the surrounding hills which take its name dominate the landscape. They do this by stealth rather than stature, creeping up onto the route in a friendly, non-threatening sort of way then staying close at hand for the duration.

Stage 4A also includes the spur into Rothbury, a very attractive small market town with various types of accommodation and well worth a visit in its own right.

Wooler and the Cheviots from Weetwood Bank

ROUTE POINTS

- **Bellingham** to **Wooler** is braided with two main route options, each with its own merit. Stage **4B** describes the northern strand which includes numerous off-road sections. The southern strand described in this chapter is more direct, always on tarmac, always open and always scenic. The ascent over Billsmoor is not as tranquil or as dramatic as the northern option, but it is still guaranteed to take your breath away.

- Best described as 'mixed and varied' this southern all-tarmac option and its continuation is always enjoyable. There are quiet **B** roads, lightly-trafficked **C** roads and little-used narrow country lanes. En route services may not be plentiful but are there when you most need them. At the time of going to press, the main route has some signed options giving access to village facilities but they have the potential to confuse unless prepared for in advance.

- The **PCW** to Alwinton and then on to **Wooler** is a delight as it girds the hills in the lee of their eastern flank all the way into **Wooler** where your rest will have been well-earned. The route description in this chapter covers the on-road route option.

BELLINGHAM

Bellingham* is the main village in the North Tyne Valley and serves a large rural hinterland. Though smaller than Haltwhistle, it too is a functional and largely self-sufficient village as far as basic requirements are concerned. On the whole, the pace of life is relaxed but some might say it is too relaxed! B&B accommodation is not thick on the ground so booking ahead is recommended. Remember to take into account that Bellingham is also a main stopover on the Reivers Cycle Route and the Pennine Way.

'Bel' is a hill, 'ing' is a meadow in a wet place and 'ham' was originally a homestead. There are a number of prefixed 'inghams' in Northumberland and they are all pronounced —ingjum as in Bellingjum.

BELLINGHAM TIC Tel: 01434 220616; Bellingham YH, Tel:

220313/Fax: 01434 220313
CYCLE SPARES (LIMITED) Village and Country Store (note the range of services advertised on the shop front!)
LOOS AND BREWS (Two tearooms), fish and chip shop, general supplies; public toilets
VISITOR ATTRACTIONS Local history interpretation at the TIC/tearoom; Heritage Centre at the old station
PLACE OF INTEREST Hareshaw Linn (a lovely wooded 2km walk from the village up to a waterfall)

PHs in remote villages are not always open. Contact details:
The Star, Harbottle (map P67) 01669 650221
The Rose & Thistle, Alwinton (map P67) 01669 650226

Starting the day with a climb is not ideal but for the all-tarmac route option this is non-negotiable. The eastbound Reivers Cycle Route shares the same road from the centre of Bellingham for just 200m before it forks R. The PCW is SA up past the YH to begin the height gain of 70m (over 2km) which is not serious but enough to raise the pulse any time of the day. The remaining distance to West Woodburn (5km) is a doddle, being either level or gently downhill. *Note: Hole Farm bastle situated close to the road on your R.* The River Rede is your companion for the next 10km (6 miles). West Woodburn, with its two pubs and shop, straddles the River Rede but more significantly it lies on the A68 which has to be crossed by means of an offset X-rds – please take care! TR then TL to join the narrow and gently winding road which is a delight, through and beyond East Woodburn as far as the A696(T) (7km). Be ready for the short sharp 50m climb out of the hamlet!

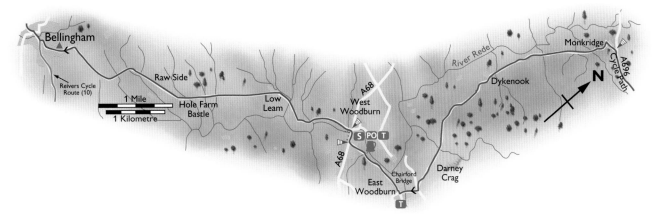

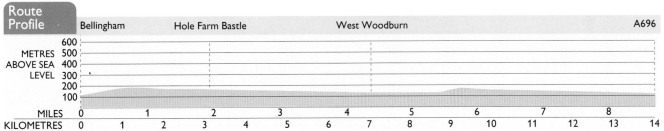

ELSDON

Elsdon is a quaint place and is thought to be one of the two most isolated village in England. (The other is Kielder on the Reivers Cycle Route 17 miles west of Bellingham.) Once the crossroads for a number of ancient highways, it quietly boasts a very well-preserved double 'motte and bailey' Norman defence (two tall earth mounds each encircled by an earthen rampart and ditch), a superb pele tower (tall, castle-like fortified house built around 1400) and a 14th century church. All of this is eclipsed by one of the most cycle-friendly tearooms in Britain (also B&B and low key TIC), situated 100m up from the PH overlooking the village green. Don't miss it! NB Public toilets are in the village hall.

TR onto the A696(T) and cycle along its metre-wide edge to Raylees Farm (1km) *Note: There is a narrowish cycle path on the south side of the road beginning at the lay-by if you prefer.* TL to the next short climb before enjoying the fast descent into Elsdon (2.5km) and the 'Impromptu' cyclists' cafe. Watch out for oncoming cars and look out at the views – in their different ways, both have significant impact potential!

Why are so many good refreshment stops followed by a steep climb! This one has a 100m height gain over 2km for which the descent is just reward. The route then undulates along the valley bottom (a total distance of 6km from Elsdon). **Warning: most weekends, this road is very popular with motorcyclists.** *Note: Look out for numerous 'holloways' curving their way up and over the hills but easily visible from the B6341. These pre-date the road by a century or two and were created by packhorse trains wearing hollows in the ground by constant passage. Well-used routes are evidenced by a series of parallel holloways.*

TL at Swindon to continue on route (go to page 66) or SA for the spur to Rothbury described overleaf.

TIP OF THE DAY   Make your gear changing smooth – only change when pedalling but not when applying full weight to the pedals on uphill sections

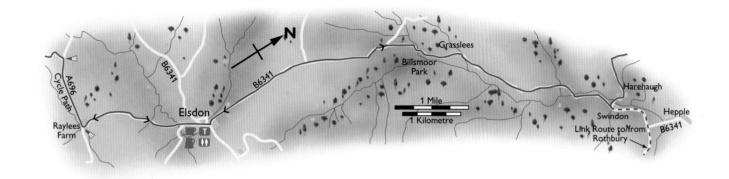

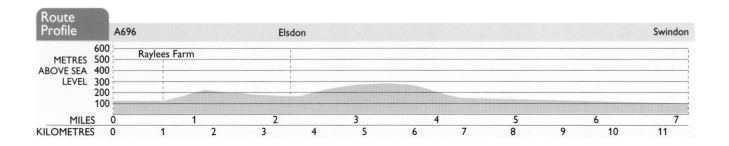

ROTHBURY

Rothbury is a sizeable village also in the small country town category. Almost all stone-built, Rothbury is made additionally attractive by its tree-lined central road on which the shops and main services are situated. Draped with daffodils in the early spring and ablaze with blossom in the late spring, Rothbury's next splash of colour lies close by in the grounds of Cragside, the National Trust property which is awash with flowering azaleas and rhododendrons in early summer. At any time of year, Rothbury and Cragside are well worth a visit.

ROTHBURY TIC (seasonal) Tel: 01669 620887 (situated in the National Park Visitor Centre)
CYCLE HIRE AND SPARES (limited): The Spar Shop, High Street, Rothbury, Tel: 01669 621338
LOOS AND BREWS Tearooms, two fish and chip shops, general supplies, several pubs
ACCOMMODATION Hotels and B&Bs
PUBLIC TRANSPORT Passenger bus service only
VISITOR ATTRACTIONS Local history and flora/fauna interpretation at the National Park Visitor Centre
PLACE OF INTEREST Cragside House (National Trust) house and grounds, Tel: 01669 620333, the home of inventor and industrialist Lord Armstrong; first domestic house in the world to be powered by electricity and just happens to be amazingly picturesque. Warning: The road route to the main entrance to Cragside is dangerous for cyclists – the obvious alternative via the very pleasant and cyclable riverside bridleway does not access a convenient paypoint so is not a lot of help (yet).

Spur to Rothbury

The main route north takes a TL at a couple of houses called Swindon. Continue SA for almost 1km then, leaving the B6341, SA along the minor road which climbs and descends towards Rothbury on the south side of the River Coquet. At Newtown TL for the off-road route into Rothbury or SA for the on-road option.

Rejoining the PCW north of Rothbury is not straightforward as the B6341 heading north-east is very definitely not recommended for cyclists and neither really is the section westward to Thropton. Should this slightly less dangerous option be used then TR at Thropton at the Cross Keys PH then after 400m TL to head directly and pleasantly to Netherton via Snitter (tearoom) thus avoiding the very steep hill up to Cartington. This area has a Cycle Routes map/guide of its own produced by the Northumberland National Park Authority with routes researched by this author. The River Coquet Source to Sea Cycle Route is yet another way of enjoying this part of the world.

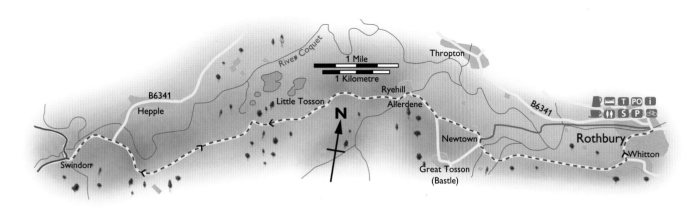

River Coquet

1 Mile

1 Kilometre

Thropton

B6341

Ryehill

Little Tosson

Allerdene

Hepple

B6341

N

Newtown

Rothbury

Swindon

Great Tosson
(Bastle)

Whitton

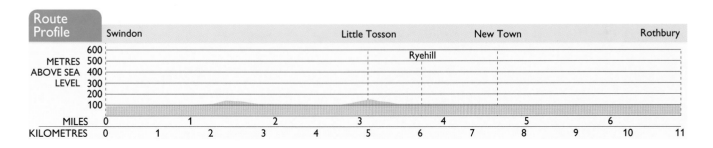

| Route Profile | Swindon | | | | | Little Tosson | | New Town | | | Rothbury |

METRES 600
ABOVE SEA 500 Ryehill
LEVEL 400
300
200
100

MILES 0 1 2 3 4 5 6

KILOMETRES 0 1 2 3 4 5 6 7 8 9 10 11

The Harbottle Stone

Main PCW Route to Alwinton (from Elsdon via the B6341): On-road

Travelling east from Elsdon TL for the most enjoyable route to Alwinton (9.5km) which follows close to the River Coquet (*pronounced Koakit*) first passing the well-preserved and accessible Woodhouses Bastle (L) followed closely by the striking Holystone Grange which shares the name of the next hamlet lying just off-route. Regrettably the PH shown on the OS map is no longer in business. *Note: Holystone is a place of sacred legend. In the 1200s a missionary preached the gospel from a 'holy' stone. Later a priory for a community of nuns was built near a sacred spring originally called Ladies' Well but now spelt Lady's Well. It is said the last wolf in Redesdale was killed in this parish at Wolf Crag and would you believe it – there is a Rob Roy's Cave near by.*

Harbottle comes next and is a little gem. This neat and tidy village has a pub, a tiny post office and the excellent Byre B&B and bunkbarn. As you cycle by, don't miss the ornate drinking fountain (now dry) in front of a charming row of cottages (R). Harbottle Castle built about 1160 is characterised by a gravity-defying wall. Stop for a few minutes and read the recently carved inscriptions around its small car park and picnic area written by local children who were asked to compare warfare in olden times with today. There are some challenging thoughts. To meet up with the northern route option,

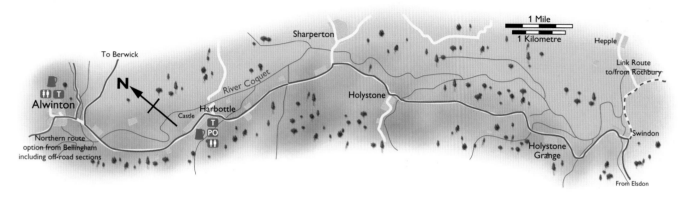

Direction of travel

To Berwick

Sharperton

1 Mile

1 Kilometre

Hepple

N

River Coquet

Alwinton

Castle

Harbottle

Holystone

Link Route to/from Rothbury

Swindon

Northern route option from Bellingham including off-road sections

Holystone Grange

From Elsdon

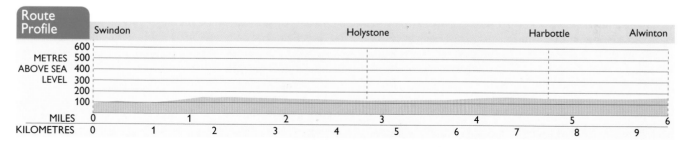

Route Profile

	Swindon	Holystone	Harbottle	Alwinton

| METRES ABOVE SEA LEVEL | 600 500 400 300 200 100 | | | |

| MILES | 0 | 1 | 2 | 3 | 4 | 5 | 6 |
| KILOMETRES | 0 | 1 | 2 | 3 | 4 | 5 | 6 | 7 | 8 | 9 |

continue ever-so-pleasantly to the small and unspoilt hamlet of Alwinton (PH with B&B) which once accommodated Sir Walter Scott whilst he was researching Rob Roy connections. 100m past the Rose and Crown PH are the public toilets.

Alwinton is where the PCW 4A (road route) intersects with PCW 4B (off-road sections). A choice of either option for the continuation route from Alwinton remains. The continuation **road route** assumes you have cycled from Harbottle into Alwinton which is situated a short distance beyond the bridge over the River Alwin. The two onward options depart either side of this bridge. Hopefully the signs will become more user-friendly in due course. For the **off-road** route option take the narrow riverside tarmac road on the north side of the River Alwin.

After coming **from** Alwinton, cross the River Alwin then TL at the grass triangle up the hill which is an ascent of 100m over 2.5km. TL after 2.5km along a much narrower road to be joined by the off-road route at the right angled corner. TR (or SA from the off-road route) to begin the section of the PCW the introduction to this chapter suggests 'girds the hills in the lee of their eastern flank'. Peddle and

enjoy but plan ahead and decide which route option you are going for.

Alwinton to the tiny hamlet of Alnham (10km) is straight forward. There is a PH in Netherton but with limited opening hours which is situated 1.5km to the south or take the off road green lane shown on page 69 which parallels the Netherton Burn from Biddlestone. At Alnham, TL off-route at the T-j for 5 minutes to take in the 13th century church with its adjacent former vicarage, a fortified house of some distinction. *Just beyond is the source of the River Aln, crossing the gateway onto Salter's Road track, the old packhorse route across the Cheviots along which this once valuable commodity was transported on its journey from coastal saltpans to inland destinations.* Continue a few more metres to the cattle grid to observe the rows of curved holloways carving their way uphill – best seen with the evening shadows or when it is frosty. *Note: Though 'ham' means a small settlement, Alnham used to be an important gateway into the Vale of Whittingham which the PCW is now entering.* It is recommended that you choose your preferred onward route option at this juncture.

TIP OF THE DAY   On topping a 'low gear' hill, maintain 'rhythm and flow' by gently moving up through the gears to increase speed without stress or undue effort to allow for recovery without stopping

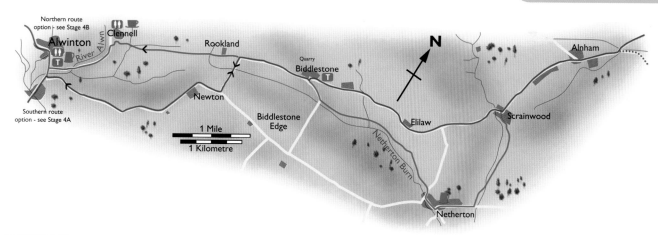

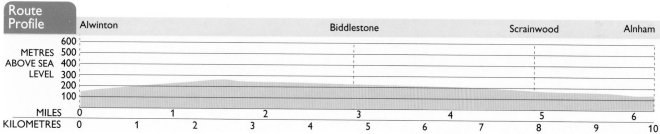

The Options

The PH shown on the OS map in Whittingham is now closed but not the one in Glanton which at the time of writing doesn't sell tea or coffee. Fortunately there is a small tearoom across the road which does when open. Powburn offers more certainty with its garage and cycle hire (essential spares); the garage shop has a cashpoint, and there is a small campsite with several chalets and a PH (teas and pub food). At Ingram there is a small National Park Visitor/Information Centre with toilets and machine-supplied refreshments. Roseden is an excellent farm shop with tearoom and meals (at busy times service can be slow) but there is an 80m ascent over 1km up an off-road track to rejoin the main PCW route to Wooler at Ilderton although the recommended on-road route to Wooler passes by the door (described on page 74).

From Alnham, the River Aln Source to Sea Cycle Route is probably the best route to the small hamlet of Branton (10.5km). 1km beyond Alnham TR then after 2km TL through Little Ryle (where there is yet another bastle house) to shadow the narrow and meandering River Aln on your L before you pass through Eslington Park. The onward and level route via Whittingham, which continues next to the still-narrow River Aln, is very pleasant but it is probably better to then TL at the east end of Eslington Park. Signed to 'Mountain', the ensuing ascent is quite forgiving being only 70m of height gain over 1km to rejoin the main PCW just before Mile End Farm. Glanton is SA and remains an option or TL to the aforementioned Branton for the quick and easy level spur to Powburn in which case TR then after 400m TR again to then carefully cross the A697 to the garage services and campsite, etc. *Note: It is legal to cycle on footways in Northumberland outside of 30mph limits.* Reverse the above to return to Branton, the small hamlet on the main route.

The signed route via Great Ryle is slightly more direct but less interesting.

Note: Branton is the hamlet south of the River Breamish whereas Brandon is the farm on the north side of the river which is crossed by a footbridge.

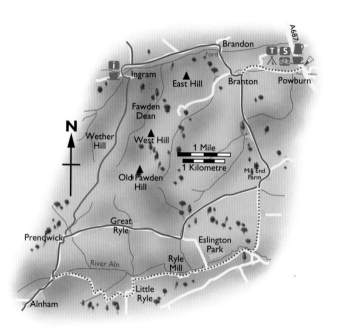

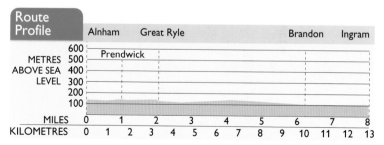

Route Profile

	Alnham	Great Ryle			Brandon	Ingram

Branton Bridge, River Breamish

Main Route (Branton to Roseden): On-road

TL at Branton (or SA from Powburn) then TR to cross the River Breamish (yet another superb Source to Sea Cycle Route) by the footbridge. TL to Ingram and the National Park Visitor and Information Centre (NPVIC) with its public toilets – only a couple of minutes off-route (3.8km from Branton). This short detour requires a TL to continue the onward route north making Ingram NPVIC to Wooler (13.2km) the last section to complete the day's ride. Apart from the odd 'slopelet', the route continues pleasantly and easily to the Ilderton Moor track junction described in Stage 4B. TR for the Roseden farm shop and tearoom option down 'the Avenue' (*note: Red squirrel sign*) to Roddam with its castellated courtyard where you TL then again TL by Roseden Farm. *Notice the enormous girth of the sycamore tree at the entrance.* On departing Roseden farm shop, TR for the uphill off-road route to Ilderton, very probably having to DAP to the hilltop. This signed option has further off-road sections – but the recommended on-road route is described next.

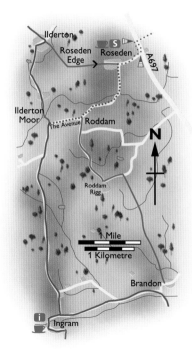

TIP OF THE DAY Horses can be spooked by bikes (see Cycling Code) – always slow right down and politely warn both rider and horse of your presence. If the horse is really spooked pull back, dismount and lay your bike flat on the ground away from the animal

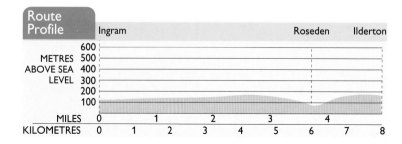

73

Roseden to Wooler

At the farm shop and tearoom entrance, TL (east) down to the A697 which is a fast main road. TL with care for 300m then with even more care TR across the traffic flow to East Lilburn. After 1.5km TL for a further 1.5km then TR over the Lilburn Burn past the entrance to Lilburn Towers (L). *This short stretch of road is where this writer once sat and watched a red squirrel dance along the full length of the top rail of the post and rail fence which borders the field (R).* SA at the T-j past Lilburntower Farm along a very quiet little used lane to eventually descend quite steeply to Haugh Head (garage, cycle hire and spares) on the A697 (3.6km from Lilburn Bridge). TR to Wooler along the unwelcoming A697 if tarmac is your preference but take care. The best option is TL through Haugh Head Farm then SA across the A697 along a good off-road track which crosses the Wooler Water by ford and footbridge. The main PCW route is up the continuation track, a mere 600m total distance from the unpleasant A697. Enjoy the freewheel into Wooler but remember to stop in time if staying at the YH (L). It would be a pity to have to cycle back uphill to your bed!

Bellingham to Wooler via Elsdon: 79km (48 miles)
TOTAL distance from Kendal: 268km (161 miles)

Chapter 4B describes the northern route option from Bellingham to Wooler via Alwinton with its through-forest off-road sections, the ascent to Dere Street (the original road across the Cheviots constructed by the Romans) and the wonderful narrow road route which threads down the Upper Coquet valley through the very core of the Cheviot Hills. It also covers recommended off-road route options between Alwinton and Wooler. This is off-road and wonderfully quiet on-road cycling at its very best – conditional on weather, energy and navigational skills.

TIP OF THE DAY   When correctly selected, your gears should not make a noise – clicks, brattles and chain jumps usually mean you are not quite in gear so press your gear lever(s) slightly or reselect your gear to cure

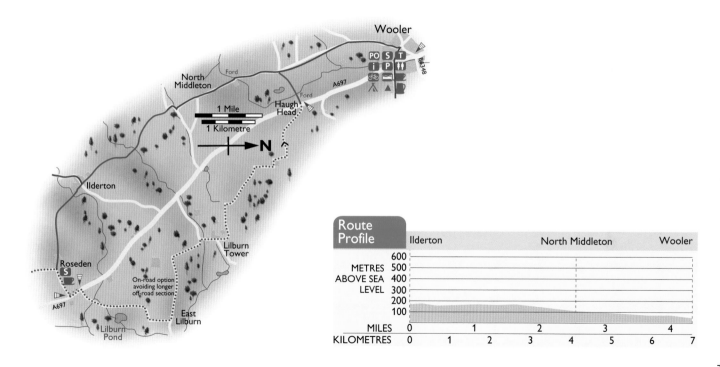

Wooler

North Middleton

Ford

Haugh Head

Ford

A697

B6348

PO S T
i P
♿ ⛺ ☕

1 Mile

1 Kilometre

N

Ilderton

Lilburn Tower

Roseden

On-road option avoiding longer off-road section.

A697

East Lilburn

Lilburn Pond

Route Profile

	Ilderton	North Middleton	Wooler

METRES ABOVE SEA LEVEL

600
500
400
300
200
100

MILES 0   1   2   3   4
KILOMETRES 0 1 2 3 4 5 6 7

OS MAPS: Landranger 80 and 81
SUSTRANS MAP: PCW (NCN Route 68 Appleby–Berwick upon Tweed)

This chapter describes what the writer believes is the most memorable part of the PCW (North). The northern upland route to Alwinton from Bellingham is an adventure! Yes it is challenging but if MOD opening times permit and the weather is kind then this route option will remain in your memory .

Country roads, winding lanes, tree-lined tracks and conifered switchbacks characterise the route as far as the A68. Once crossed, the forest is soon left behind and the climb on narrow tarmac up and over Northumberland's only 'mountain' pass begins. The summit is a plateau with commanding views leading to a thrilling descent down to Chew Green Roman camp after which begins the superb descent of the Upper River Coquet Valley. All the way to Alwinton, the narrow road literally hugs the banks of the river just occasionally surmounting the odd steep shoulder of hillside.

Upper Coquetdale in the Cheviots

ROUTE POINTS

- The first half of this stage describes the partially off-road northern route to Alwinton. **PLEASE NOTE: The route passes through a Ministry of Defence training area with restricted opening times. If you take this option it is essential to check road open dates and times in advance, but no later than Bellingham.**

- It is impossible to fully appreciate the total experience offered by the **PCW** without completing the on- and off-road section which leads to the Upper River Coquet watershed.

- It goes without saying that it is not recommended to cycle along any section of the **A68.**

- The route from Alwinton to Wooler **IS** a delight as it girds the eastern lee of the Cheviots. Nearer Wooler, the main route for the PCW follows some sections of off-road tracks but the road options described in this chapter offer a very pleasant alternative.

THE REIVERS

In the 15th and 16th centuries, the Scottish border with England was often fought over and re-positioned many times. A wide area of the 'borderlands' became known as the 'debatables'. Reivers is the name given to the numerous family clans who inhabited those lands and whose survival depended on frequent raids to plunder and steal from their lowland neighbours. Often these incursions lasted a number of weeks and many miles were travelled on horseback as violent battles for land and animals prevailed. Numerous fortifications were built including bastle houses (fortified farmsteads with very thick walls and a vaulted cellar into which animals were driven if warning was given). Many people were killed in these raids and those surviving were said to be 'bereaved'. There are accounts of some Reivers wearing a type of dark mail for protection. Just the sight of the Reivers so clad sometimes 'persuaded' farmers to give them their animals to avoid loss of human life. Such victims were then said to have been 'blackmailed'.

This PCW northern option, which includes numerous, fine off-road sections, leaves Bellingham by the arrival route of Stage 3 which shares the Reivers Cycle Route (RCR) signed with a number 10 on a blue background. Cross the North Tyne west of Bellingham on the B6320 after which TR to the T-j at Dunterley then continue SA. Quite unusually, the OS 80 Landranger map has the status of the two riverside roads the wrong way round. The road along the southern bank is the quiet, narrow and much more scenic road whilst on the northern side the C200 road is much straighter, wider, busier and faster – the motorbikers love it. After a very pleasant 6.5km TR to recross the river then up to Lanehead where the RCR takes a TL. As well as being part of the Reivers Cycle Route, the recommended link route west to Falstone and Kielder Water also forms part of the River North Tyne Source to Sea CR .

Kielder Water lies some 8 miles to the west of the PCW off-road northern route option which is described in this chapter. The Reivers Cycle Route and like all the Source to Sea Cycle Routes referred to in this book, was also created and surveyed by this author. The route between Lanehead and the lake is very quiet and extremely pleasant. Falstone is a pretty little village with a PH and a tearoom – the map for this route extension is located on page 91 at the end of this chapter.

Direction of travel

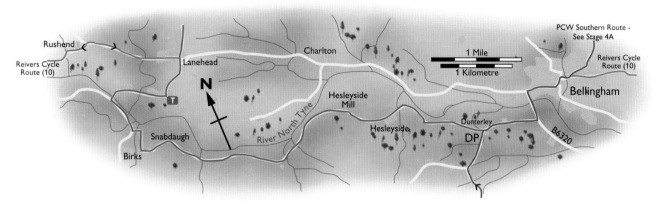

PCW Southern Route -
See Stage 4A

Reivers Cycle
Route (10)

Rushend

Reivers Cycle
Route (10)

Charlton

1 Mile

1 Kilometre

Lanehead

Bellingham

N

Hesleyside
Mill

River North Tyne

Dunterley

B6320

Snabdaugh

Hesleyside

DP

Birks

Route Profile

Bellingham	Hesleyside	River North Tyne (bridge)	Lanehead

METRES	600
ABOVE SEA	500
LEVEL	400
	300
	200
	100

MILES: 0 1 2 3 4 5

KILOMETRES: 0 1 2 3 4 5 6 7 8 9

79

TAKE NOTE!

It is this next section to Chew Green [10km] that requires MOD clearance before you set off but, obviously, this has to be ascertained well before arriving at this point. Bellingham is the last place to do this. Telephone 0191 261 1046 and ask for the Range Liaison office for this information. Road open times are often known quite a long time in advance and because it is so worthwhile including this northern option in your itinerary, the only way of being really sure is to research the 'road open' dates and then consider making your off-road PCW route plans around those dates. At the time of writing, there are close to 100 days a year when this route is open. Weekends are usually open but not in every case whilst bank holidays are rarely closed. Mid April to mid May is always open due to lambing and maintenance. It is anticipated that the number of 'road open' dates will be increased in due course. One further option is to look into the possibility of cycling from the A68 to Alwinton after 5pm during the light nights when the Chew Green section is often open. Please telephone in advance whatever time of year and day you are considering cycling this section of the route. You will not regret this extra effort.

SA to Greenhaugh and the Holly Bush PH and B&B with limited opening hours (Tel: 01434 240391), the last watering hole for quite some time (10km from Bellingham). Soon after, TR to cross the Tarret Burn. *Note: the parallel packhorse 'holloways' curving up the hillside adjacent to the road.* At the next T-j, TR to once again cross the Tarret Burn before the climb up past Highgreen Manor [100m height gain over 1.3km] then TL along a very narrow road leading into even more remote terrain. SA past Gibbshiel (*shiel means a shelter*) then continue between the trees along the gently ascending track which at its highest point (347m) shares the alignment of the Pennine Way [9.5km from the Holly Bush). Just take in the views!

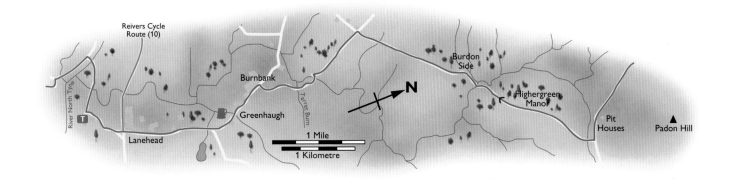

Reivers Cycle
Route (10)

River North Tyne

Burnbank

Greenhaugh

Lanehead

Tarret Burn

N

1 Mile

1 Kilometre

Burdon
Side

Highergreen
Manor

Pit
Houses

▲
Padon Hill

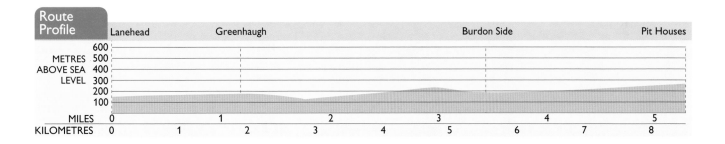

Route Profile

	Lanehead	Greenhaugh	Burdon Side	Pit Houses

METRES
ABOVE SEA
LEVEL

600
500
400
300
200
100

MILES   0   1   2   3   4   5

KILOMETRES   0   1   2   3   4   5   6   7   8

View of the army road looking back to Byrness

For the aggressively confident cyclists, the switchback that follows is a test of bumps, balance and bottle. For everyone else it is a matter of grin, grip and grind but whichever category you belong to – don't be put off a) choosing this route and b) your cycle whilst on it! The now wide forest track drops down to the Forest Drive toll road at the 200m contour [3km] where there are public toilets at the picnic site. TL along the Forest Drive track then after 200m, TR keeping the River Rede on your R. Look out for Cottonshopeburnfoot across the river. *Note: With 19 letters, this is the longest place name in England.* TR to cross the R Rede then DAP immediately after the bridge along a short section of footpath to access a narrow but functional crossing point of the aforementioned burn (stream) which leads into the Border Forest Camping and Caravan site with its own bunkhouse (Tel: 01830 520259) less than 2km from the toll road.

After periods of heavy rain, the burn may be difficult to cross in which case keep SA to join the A68 then TL for 300m (take great care) to the above-described Border Forest site. For the off-road route to Byrness YH (*pronounced burrness with stronger emphasis on the 'ness'*), TL before crossing the R Rede then next TR down to the ford and footbridge soon after which TL along yet another forest track to the YH (2km). There is a tearoom at the nearby fuel station. **Warning: The A68 is a very fast road along which it is not recommended to cycle.** *Note: The River Rede is the ideal location to rest awhile before tackling the next section!*

Direction of travel

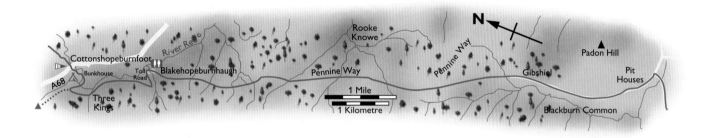

N

Cottonshopeburnfoot
Bunkhouse
Toll Road
Blakehopeburnhaugh
A68
Three Kings
River Rede
Rooke Knowe
Pennine Way
Pennine Way
Gibshiel
Padon Hill
Pit Houses
Blackburn Common

1 Mile
1 Kilometre

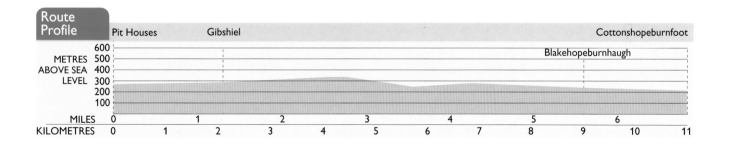

Route Profile

| | Pit Houses | Gibshiel | | | | Cottonshopeburnfoot |

| METRES ABOVE SEA LEVEL | | | | | | Blakehopeburnhaugh |

600
500
400
300
200
100

| MILES | 0 | | 1 | | 2 | | 3 | | 4 | | 5 | | 6 | |
| KILOMETRES | 0 | 1 | 2 | 3 | 4 | 5 | 6 | 7 | 8 | 9 | 10 | 11 |

From the Border Forest Park Caravan and camp site:

The route to Alwinton is all on narrow tarmac for which the section over Cottonshopeburn Head is remarkably smooth. Cross the A68 with care using the cycle lanes provided then SA between the trees which are soon left behind being replaced by increasing open and wild countryside – ideal terrain for toughening up and training an army. Hopefully your carefully pre-planned day is warm and sunny with a pleasant tailwind (and if pigs could fly then bacon would go up). The 'pass' is not too rigorous as there is a long easy approach but the steep section is a pulse-raiser for sure. Ascending 500m over 8km is not difficult although the steepest bit is 110m height gain over 1km. Like the climb, on a clear day the panoramic views are breathtaking.

After the steep section, TL at Middle Golden Pot for the summit plateau ride along Dere Street which is one of the oldest highways (literally) in Britain. This is an amazing fact considering its exposed location. *Note: This section of route is also called Gamel's Path named after a tribal leader who lived locally some time after the demise of the Roman empire.* Just after Outer Golden Pot, and if time and elements allow, stop at spot height 510 to take in the view before beginning the steep and potentially dangerous breakpad-wearing descent to Chew Green Roman camp. **Warning: Beware loose gravel on the road and part way down there is a very** deceptive right-hand half bend which if missed would almost certainly spoil your day, your bike and your body – not recommended being absolutely miles from anywhere.

A68 to Chew Green – alternative off-road route for the fit and the experienced in good visibility!

There is an alternative off-road route between the A68 and Chew Green which is outside MOD restrictions but it is not recommended for inexperienced individuals/parties. The last and most exposed section can be almost impassable after an extended period of rain and it should be avoided by everyone in bad weather. Though waymarked, this route should not be attempted without suitable clothing and equipment associated with mountain journeys and, of course, the knowledge of how and when to use both. A compass and whistle with the associated knowledge is essential for this route in all but the finest weather. If you have the appropriate skills and experience and you thrive on challenge and adventure on your cycle with the possibility of ample measures of soggy peat thrown in for fun then go for it!

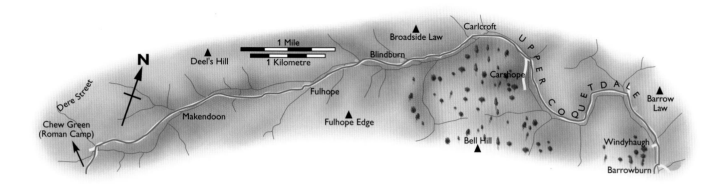

Deel's Hill

1 Mile

1 Kilometre

N

Dere Street

Makendoon

Chew Green
(Roman Camp)

Fulhope

Fulhope Edge

Blindburn

Broadside Law

Carlcroft

U P P E R   C O Q U E T D A L E

Carshope

Bell Hill

Barrow
Law

Windyhaugh

Barrowburn

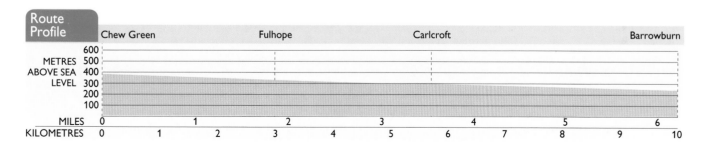

Route Profile

	Chew Green	Fulhope	Carlcroft	Barrowburn

METRES ABOVE SEA LEVEL

600
500
400
300
200
100

MILES   0   1   2   3   4   5   6

KILOMETRES   0   1   2   3   4   5   6   7   8   9   10

CHEW GREEN

Chew Green is amazing. Stop and read the roadside interpretation panel at the very least. Time permitting, wander up the short distance to the camp itself and savour the setting. Look back up your descent route and you will see the ubiquitous parallel packhorse holloways curving up the hillside. The really observant will be able to pick out the original alignment of Dere Street which entered the camp through the main gate, now just a sod-covered gap in the boundary of surviving earthworks.

Specialist off-road route avoiding MOD restrictions (Landranger 80)
SA after crossing the A68 as previously described then after 1km TL past the barrier along the third forest track on your L some 150m before the edge of the forest. This ascends almost continually but rarely steeply to the 450m contour over a distance of 4.5km to a sharp L turn in the track (GR 773 072). This is signed 'Border Ride', a long distance equestrian route created for experienced endurance riders. TR (north-east) along a narrow but mostly cyclable stone-based track through the trees to a bridle gate at the edge of the forest (500m). **Warning: The next 2km are often boggy and may be uncyclable if the weather is bad and the ground is wet.**

With the forest on your L, descend to the boundary fence north of which lies Scotland. SA (north) through the gate for 400m keeping the post and wire fence on your L, a distance of 1km from the bridle gate to cover the worst of the ground conditions. TR (signpost) and head due east for a further kilometre along an improving bridleway path to reach the western boundary of Chew Green Roman camp. Take in the setting *(see road route description on page 84)* then descend to the tarmac road and interpretation panel. **Warning: from the boundary fence do not attempt to follow the shallow valley on your R (which is in fact the source of the River Coquet) as it is very boggy but in clear weather it is a useful visual 'handrail' to use as you contour to Chew Green.** The A68 to Chew Green via this route is exactly 10km.

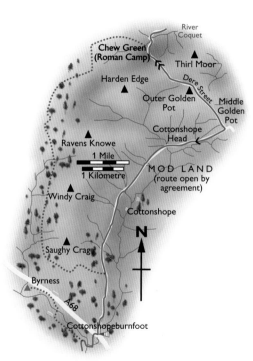

The MOD road between the A68 and Chew Green has restricted opening times. There is an alternative route which avoids this road but it is recommended for use by experienced cyclists only when conditions are clear.

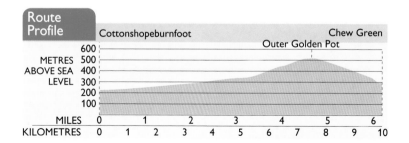

Alwinton

Follow the minor road to Alwinton [18.5km] right next to the river which wends and winds its way through the rounded Cheviot hills. There are some short sharp ascents to surmount several shoulders of hillside but even so, and given a fine day, this section of the PCW is an absolute delight!

Alwinton is where the PCW 4A (road route) intersects with PCW 4B (off-road sections). A choice of either option for the continuation route from Alwinton remains. The continuation **road route** assumes you have cycled the short distance from Alwinton to the bridge over the River Alwin. The two onward options depart either side of this bridge. For the road route see page 68.

For the **off-road** option, take the narrow riverside tarmac road on the north side of the River Alwin via Clennel Hall, a camping and caravan site with licensed premises. Fork R through the main gates into Clennel Hall keeping R towards the toilet block (which cyclists are welcome to use by kind permission of the owners). Just beyond the toilets, go through the full-size field gate in the nearby boundary wall then TR on the track to which it connects. Soon the track makes a fairly steep ascent of the hillside (DAP) with fine views at the top. Continue NE along the obvious grass track past Rookland Farm to join a narrow tarmac country lane which is the road route from Alwinton.

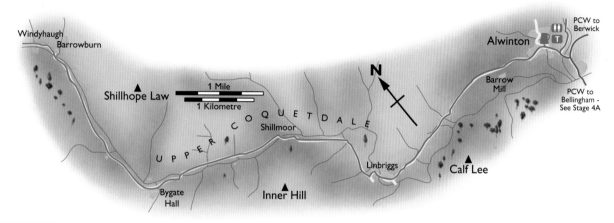

Windyhaugh
Barrowburn
Shillhope Law
1 Mile
1 Kilometre
UPPER COQUETDALE
Shillmoor
Bygate Hall
Inner Hill
Linbriggs
Calf Lee
Barrow Mill
Alwinton
PCW to Berwick
PCW to Bellingham - See Stage 4A
N

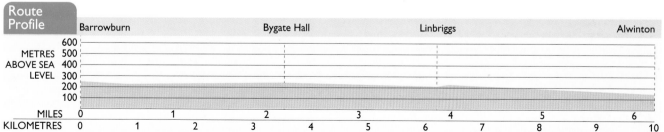

Route Profile

	Barrowburn	Bygate Hall	Linbriggs	Alwinton

METRES ABOVE SEA LEVEL
600
500
400
300
200
100

MILES 0 1 2 3 4 5 6
KILOMETRES 0 1 2 3 4 5 6 7 8 9 10

Off-road: Prendwick to Ingram

Go through the full-size gate (L) at the right-angle turn in the road then TR below the edge of the wood (R). This is an unclassified road which is very straightforward to follow for its full length of 4km. With very much a green lane surface, the track climbs at first then gently angles its way to the highest point, offering superb views of the surrounding area before the exhilarating descent to Ingram. *Remember to open (and close) the several gates on this route.* The National Park Visitor Centre is close to where this route joins the road.

Off-road: Brandon to Roddam

After leaving the National Park Visitor Centre TR to cross the River Breamish then SA to Brandon on the minor road. After the road turns L just past the footbridge (main route) continue SA up the obvious unsurfaced track for 2km which starts with the farm (R). When narrow tarmac is reached TL through the gates then after

TIP OF THE DAY   Jumping chain? Check for damage to chainset and rear sprockets; a stiff link which won't flatten out (flex chain sideways with hand grip and thumb pressure); damaged link about to snap (stop and check link by link – also look for rivet displacement)

450m TR very pleasantly to Roddam. The last section is a public road despite the private-looking gates. For the off-road continuation described next, TL just beyond the farm along The Avenue. *Note the interesting old post-box built into the wall at Roddam.* Alternatively it is SA for Roseden farm shop and tearoom and the on-road route to Wooler described in Stage 4.

Off-road: The Avenue (west of Roddam) to North Middleton (Map page 75)

The wide track heading north from where The Avenue turns east soon narrows to a short steep section of holloway which once carried horse and carriages bound for Edinburgh. It is stoney rough but only for a short distance down to the picturesque ford and footbridge. The uphill path soon relents and improves as the minor road to Ilderton is reached. TL at the farm where the off-road route from Roseden comes in from the R. The next very scenic 2.5kms is off-road and of mixed quality but cyclable for most bikes. Take care to TL after the next footbridge and ford over the Lilburn Burn - do not continue between the incongruous parallel row of trees following the direction of the stream. One last ford with an upstream footbridge appears some 1 km after tarmac is regained for the last time beyond which are public loos close to the next TL. SA for an easy ride into Wooler.

**Reivers Cycle Route (10) and
link route to/from Kielder Water**

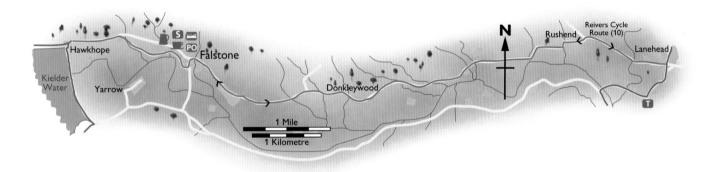

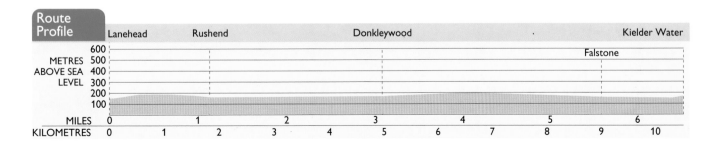

OS MAP: Landranger 75

SUSTRANS MAP: PCW (NCN Route 68 Appleby–Berwick upon Tweed)

The route from Wooler to Berwick upon Tweed is a real pleasure. Watching the hills grow smaller as slopelets and undulations take over from granny rings and grunts may please the tired legs but surely it will sadden the hearts of those who have come to love, and even sometimes hate, those wonderful contours.

This is the final chapter in the book and, in the way of all good books, the plot continues to unfold right to the end. Flat sections are enlivened by eye-catching locations; surprises are around some of the most unlikely corners and often when least expected. These last few miles are increasingly easy and hugely enjoyable but never an anticlimax. Enjoy to the very last pedal turn.

Berwick upon Tweed

ROUTE POINTS

- The hills are left behind but not forgotten as the **PCW** heads to its conclusion and the border town of Berwick upon Tweed. The terrain and the landscape undergo a remarkable transformation as the route follows a series of tranquil lanes, wider minor roads and quiet B roads.
- Ford, Heatherslaw and Etal are the first surprises with their castles, light railway, working flour mill and thatched roofs. Hamlets and unspoilt villages like Horncliffe and Paxton come and go and the ambiance becomes distinctly relaxed and unhurried as the miles pass by.
- Norham, a border town with yet another castle precedes the unusual Chain (suspension) Bridge over the River Tweed leading into Scotland close to Paxton House. The familiar green horizon turns a shimmering but distant blue as the North Sea finally comes into view.
- The **PCW** ends with a gentle downhill towards the town centre, the nearby harbour and finally the north pier – the end of the journey and the end of an adventure.

WOOLER

Wooler is a rural community which relies largely on its own endeavours – a truism which probably extends back to its earliest days. It is yet another unpretentious hybrid country town which is too big to be a village and too small to be a rural town. Some describe stone-built Wooler as austere which it may be architecturally but 'functional' is probably more apt in terms of its location and history. Along with the other market towns on the PCW, Wooler is also self-sufficient which reflects positively on the people who live there and have its interest at heart. The local accent more than hints at Wooler's proximity to Scotland. Friendly people providing value for money services makes Wooler a good place to be.

WOOLER TIC 01668 282123 (situated in the National Park Visitor Centre and combined Community Centre in Padgepool Place); public toilets

CYCLE HIRE AND SPARES (limited) Fergusons Motors and Cycles, Tel: 01668 281316, situated 2km south of Wooler on the busy A697

LOOS AND BREWS Tearooms, fish and chip shops, general supplies, several pubs; public toilets

ACCOMMODATION Full range of hotels and B&Bs, two campsites and Wooler YH, Tel: 01668 281365 Fax: 01668 282368

PUBLIC TRANSPORT Passenger bus service only

VISITOR ATTRACTIONS Local history and interpretation at the National Park Visitor Centre, Padgepool Place

It is a long straight and predictable road which leads northwards from Wooler directly to Berwick upon Tweed. Most of the day, the B6525 is relatively quiet but what vehicles do use it invariably travel in 'fast and furious' mode particularly to and from work. The straight road to Doddington [4km] not only hits the traffic but misses the point – a little further on the 'quiet and the narrow' provides a better experience than the fast, the straight and the direct. Fast and predictable are two things the slightly longer route is NOT with its relaxed feel and Cheviot views. It has been chosen as a much safer and more enjoyable alternative.

From the main street, descend The Peth to cross the A697 to then pass Glendale Middle School. *Note: A 'peth' is a road or a path on a hill as in Morpeth and Brancepeth.* After 800m TL to soon TR on the quiet B6348 which leads to the listing but rather beautiful Weetwood bridge over the River Till. TL then again TL onto narrow Sandy Lane which contours Weetwood Hill remembering to throw wistful glances towards the receding Cheviots (L) for not many hills lie ahead. TR onto the hitherto avoided B6525 to cycle into Doddington (7 pleasant kilometres from Wooler). *Note: The large number of 'cup and ring' rocks marked on the Landranger 75 map on the low hills to the east. The local rock is hard sandstone on which a central cup with concentric rings has been carved by ancient people for no known reason. These markings have been discovered all over the*

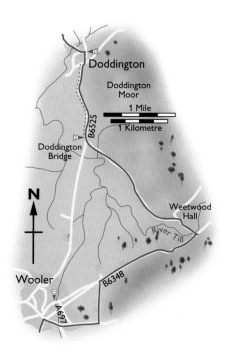

TIP OF THE DAY Read the route ahead – beware gravel, running water, leaves, rain and slippy surfaces especially on corners

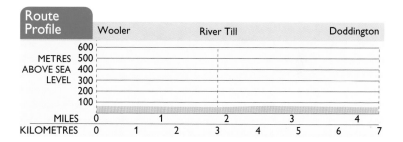

MILFIELD PLAIN

This alluvial plain, with its inevitable sand and gravel extraction, was deposited millions of years ago in the post-glacial period. There have been some fascinating 'finds' in this area with further hidden treasures thought to be awaiting discovery.

Milfield airstrip is now used by a glider club but its wartime function was as a training base for a constant stream of trainee pilots from the UK and abroad. The remains of at least one Lancaster bomber can still be seen on Cheviot itself!

Milfield wood henge is a 3km detour. It is a full-scale reproduction of a stone-age henge, a typical replica of the many henges which stood in this landscape 4300 years ago. It is free to visit and the time trail is most enjoyable – optional trail guides available from Milfield Country Cafe and Store but take care on the A697. There is a permissive off-road route through Floddenford Plantation to Ford which off-road cyclists will enjoy.

world but they proliferate in this part of Northumberland. TL to Fenton.

Milfield Plain on your L lies in sharp contrast to the still-obvious Cheviot hills which rim the horizon to the south.

Main route – Fenton to Ford, Heatherslaw and Etal

At Fenton TR then after 1km TL via Kimmerston Riding stables to Ford village [5km]. TR up to the old church (L) to absorb enough history to fill a book: *14th century Ford Castle, now a field study and residential centre; Ford Nursery in the two-acre Victorian walled garden; the extremely picturesque stone-built Ford village (a 'model' estate village); Lady Waterford Hall which is probably one of the most amazing village halls anywhere with its beautiful Waterford murals depicting well-known biblical scenes painted by Lady Waterford in 1862/63 and the Horseshoe Forge with its superb horseshoe doorway, now producing sculpture and hand-painted items.* To visit the above in the above-recommended order, TL along the entrance drive to Ford Castle as far as the main gate to peep into the past. TR onto the informal gravelled drive to the nursery and the village. After visiting in this manner, the return to the PCW on the B6354 is very much downhill!

SA to Heatherslaw with its 15-inch gauge light railway, original style water-powered corn mill working for demonstration and local use, the Granary Cafe, Visitor Centre, cycle hire and public toilets (Tel: 01890

Direction of travel

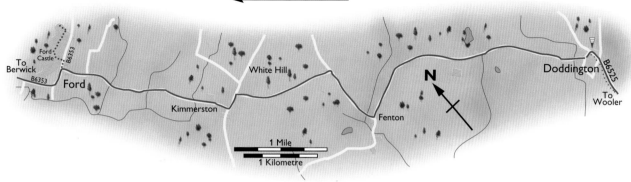

Route Profile	Doddington			Fenton		Kimmerston			Ford

METRES ABOVE SEA LEVEL	600 500 400 300 200 100								
MILES	0	1		2		3		4	5
KILOMETRES	0	1	2	3	4	5	6	7	8

820 338 for more info). Well worth a stop but if it is a wet day then cycle over the metal bridge with care!

Etal (*pronounced eetle*) is the next lovely surprise. The post office shop has a tearoom, the thatched Black Bull PH offers good food and further down from haunting 14th century Etal Castle with its audio tour facilities is Etal ford and furniture makers. The banks of the River Till offer lovely picnic spots. A little downstream stand the remains of the pedestrian suspension bridge whilst slightly upstream is the severed mill race being just one of many on the Till which were destroyed in WW2 to prevent likely invaders from harnessing the river's energy to make flour and/or tools which must have seemed a good idea at the time.

Etal to Norham

Return to the quiet B6354 then TL for almost 2km to cycle along even quieter minor roads taking with you good memories of several interesting stop-offs. Longer-stay visitors should take in Flodden Field battlesite (AD1513) via Crookham for the best X-ing of the A697. *En route to Norham, count the farm cottage chimneys at Grindon to see how many workers would once have been employed on this arable farm estate.* Cross the A698 with care to continue to Norham; do call at the old station house on your L, now a small railway museum, if it is open. TL into timeless Norham [9km from Etal] with its village green, village store (L) (hot drinks on request),

public toilets and imposing castle. *Note the pinnacled market cross set on a base of six 13th century steps. The windvane is a fish and represents the salmon industry for which the nearby River Tweed is famed. Those interested in churches will be impressed by the Norman architecture and history of the large dignified church built on the site of a building founded in the year 830. The beech-tree encircled castle, constructed on a hill by the Tweed, draws the eye with its lofty Norman keep – one of England's finest.* The PCW now joins yet another superb Source to Sea Cycle Route – the River Tweed.

This is where the PCW meets up with NCN Route 1 to/from Edinburgh as the signs now indicate. TR down the main street towards the castle but be ready to change down some gears for the steep little 'click' (colloquial for a short hill) on which it stands. After the next not-the-most-interesting 3km of the entire route, TL in the knowledge that relief is not far ahead for in only 1km is the positively somnambulent village of Horncliffe. Relief because there are public toilets and because there is a PH which serves food at certain times of the week – even more relief for the hungry or thirsty if it is open for business. Return to the main route and TL past Horncliffe House after which TL past the Honey Farm (visitors welcome) down to the Union Chain Bridge over the River Tweed. This is a very special structure so take a minute to read the inscribed information plaque mounted on the distinctive red sandstone headwall before crossing over into Scotland.

Direction of travel

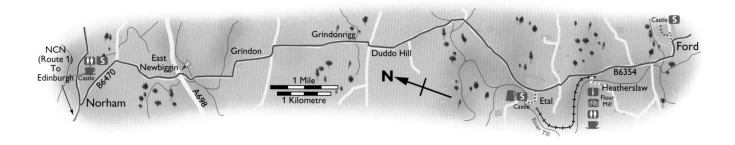

NCN
(Route 1)
To
Edinburgh

Castle

Norham

B6470

East
Newbiggin

A698

Grindon

Grindonrigg

Duddo Hill

1 Mile

1 Kilometre

N

Heatherslaw
Flour
Mill

B6354

Castle

Etal

River Till

Castle S

Ford

Route Profile		Ford		Etal					Grindon			Norham
METRES ABOVE SEA LEVEL	600											
	500											
	400											
	300											
	200											
	100											
MILES	0		1		2		3		4	5	6	7
KILOMETRES	0	1	2	3	4	5	6	7	8	9	10	11	12

The onward road has an interesting feature provided by the soft sandstone wall on your R which has been eroded by wind and rain. At its end, the road bears L to join the B6461 then TR towards Paxton. Alternatively, SA through the bridle gate is Lover's Lonnen, a pleasant old off-road track to the B6461 (TR) but take care across the old bridge midway. *Note: Lonnen, lonning, loaning or loan are all corruptions of the word 'lane'.* At the entrance to Paxton House [11km from Norham], TL into peaceful Paxton (PH) or SA towards Berwick upon Tweed and the A1(T) some 4km east of Paxton. Look for the cycle route crossing point of the A1 to your L which has been especially created for the NCN. Even so, it should be used with great care and attention.

The old road at the other side (east) of the trunk road is now a farm lane (TL) and once opposite the farm access bridge over the A1 on your L, cycle around the soil barrier close to the RH end to join Paxton Road. SA to the A6105 and TR along Castle Terrace into the residential outskirts of Berwick upon Tweed soon to join the busier North Road at the next fork. Cross the mainline railway with the station (R). [It has a one way traffic system to/from the station and once there, access to the southbound platform necessitates carrying your cycle up one set of steps and down another. *Whilst engaged in this process, give yourself time to glance at the fine Victorian masonry and wrought-iron work.*]

But the real finish is the end of the pier. Continue SA into the centre of Berwick along Castlegate, passing under Scotchgate, the old town wall gateway, and try to come to terms with the hither and thither and hustle and bustle of civilisation as the people of Berwick upon Tweed experience it. Continue SA at the main junction with the Royal Tweed Bridge and after passing the old town hall (L) on Marygate, TR down Hide Hill and then TL along Silver Ness, a residential road which leads to Pier Road and the start of the north pier, the end of your journey and for many, perhaps, the trip of a lifetime.

Alternative off-road finish

There is a magnificent and legal off-road route into Berwick which, with appropriate care, provides the quality finish this fine long distance cycle route truly deserves. Some 250m after the soil barrier where Paxton Road takes a little dip by a slight RH bend (gravel expanse opposite (L)), there is signed but very easy-to-miss narrow path which is in fact a UCR. *Note: Unclassified County Roads, of which in the UK there are literally thousands, are now being marked on recent editions of the OS maps but not all by any means. They represent the hidden network of some of Britain's finest and forgotten off-road tracks for which Local Highway Departments have responsibility but no money and therefore very little interest.* TR and descend this 'path' with care as it is prone to washout damage after prolonged heavy rain.

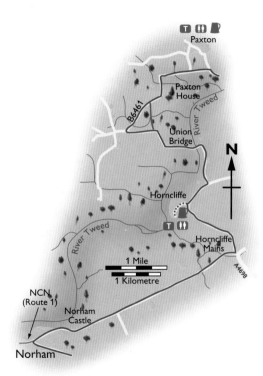

Paxton

Paxton House

Union Bridge

B6461

River Tweed

N

Horncliffe

Horncliffe Mains

A698

River Tweed

1 Mile

1 Kilometre

NCN (Route 1)

Norham Castle

Norham

TIP OF THE DAY Avoid skidding – it is the sign of misjudgement and causes excessive tyre, brake and rim wear with potential for human damage

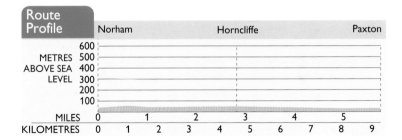

Route Profile	Norham	Horncliffe	Paxton

| METRES ABOVE SEA LEVEL | 600 500 400 300 200 100 | | |

| MILES | 0 | 1 | 2 | 3 | 4 | 5 |
| KILOMETRES | 0 | 1 | 2 | 3 | 4 | 5 | 6 | 7 | 8 | 9 |

BERWICK UPON TWEED

BERWICK TIC: 01289 330733
(situated near Scotsgate Arch on
Castlegate)
CYCLE HIRE AND SPARES: Brilliant
Bicycles, Bridge Street Tel: 01289
331476
LOOS AND BREWS: Tearooms, fish
and chip shops, pizzerias, shops of all
types, pubs; public toilets
ACCOMMODATION: Full range of
hotels and B&Bs; campsite;
bunkhouse
PUBLIC TRANSPORT: mainline
railway station plus passenger bus
service
VISITOR ATTRACTIONS: Berwick
upon Tweed Barracks, town walls,
Regimental Museum, Tower House
Pottery, The Maltings Arts Centre

Warning: Slow down when the River Tweed comes into view and prepare for a tight TL.

This too is a UCR but narrow in places so please warn others of your presence and give way to all pedestrians. The route now passes several 'shielings' (riverside shelters used by the salmon fishermen), as it winds towards the mouth of the river and the border town of Berwick upon Tweed. Slow right down to savour the next 2km. On your R is the river; best seen at high tide but always interesting. Ahead of you are the descending ramparts of old Berwick's defensive walls which still wrap themselves protectively around the heart of the town. The way through is only revealed at the last moment. Ahead is the huge and majestic multi-arched Royal Border Bridge over which runs the mainline railway and under which this route passes. Ahead is The Royal Tweed Bridge. Cycle under and onward. Ahead is the superb stone-built and solid King James the First Berwick Bridge. Just after the north end of this bridge, TR along Bridge Street then SA along Silver Ness onto Pier Road to end your ride where land finishes and the north pier starts.

Ahead, sadly, is where this adventure ends. Ahead, fortunately, is where and when the next one begins. Start planning!

Wooler to Berwick: 47km (28 miles)
TOTAL distance from Kendal: 315km (189 miles)

The end

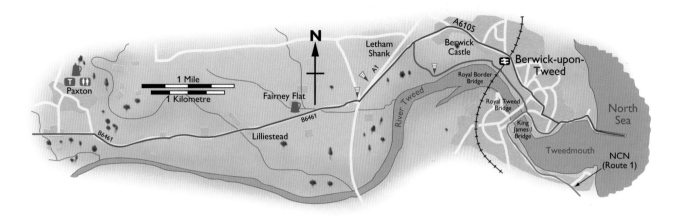

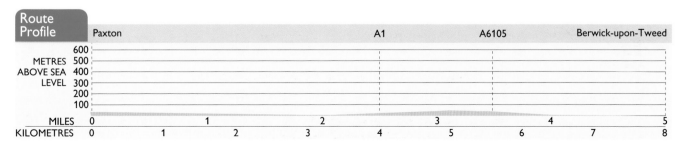

Pennine Cycleway (South)

The Pennine Cycleway (South) is the southern part of the PCW (N) and is also NCN Route 68. It begins at Derby and threads it way into and through the Peak District, the South Pennines and the Yorkshire Dales to Kendal where this guidebook begins. A direct link with the PCW (N) is possible east of the Howgills to join the route from Kendal not far from Kirkby Stephen in Cumbria. The southern half of the PCW is also a superb journey by pedal power. The route is different in character to the PCW (N) but passes through wonderful scenery and countless picturesque villages. The PCW (S) has some steep hills along the way as you would expect from the route outline but don't let that put you off – cycle the route and continue the adventure!

Other cycle routes in this region

NCN Route 1 which is also known as the Coast & Castles Cycle Route (C&C), extends down the magnificent Northumbrian coastline to Tyneside for a distance of 80 miles. The leg between Tynemouth and Haltwhistle is NCN Route 72 and this will be known as Hadrian's Cycleway (HCW) when fully open between the mouth of the Tyne and Ravenglass on the West Coast of Scotland. When HCW is combined with the PCW and the C&C CR, the resulting triangle forms a cycle tour of Northumberland which has been given the name

Northumbria's Cycling Kingdom. NB All the above mentioned CRs were originated and surveyed by this author and implemented (with some route changes) by Sustrans.

The National Cycle Network

The Pennine Cycleway is part of The National Cycle Network – a comprehensive network of safe and attractive places to cycle throughout the UK. 10,000 miles are due for completion by 2005, one third of which will be on traffic-free paths, the rest will follow quiet lanes or traffic-calmed roads. It is co-ordinated by Sustrans, with the generous support of over 450 local authorities and other partners. For more information on routes in your area, contact: Sustrans, 35 King Street, Bristol BS1 4DZ. Tel: 0845 113 0065, www.nationalcyclenetwork.org.uk.